EXHUMING
VIOLENT
HISTORIES

EXHUMING VIOLENT HISTORIES

FORENSICS, MEMORY, AND REWRITING SPAIN'S PAST

NICOLE ITURRIAGA

Columbia University Press *New York*

Columbia University Press
Publishers Since 1893
New York Chichester, West Sussex
cup.columbia.edu

Library of Congress Cataloging-in-Publication Data
Names: Iturriaga, Nicole, author.
Title: Exhuming violent histories : forensics, memory, and rewriting
Spain's past / Nicole Iturriaga.
Description: New York, NY : Columbia University Press, [2022] |
Includes bibliographical references and index.
Identifiers: LCCN 2021034728 (print) | LCCN 2021034729 (ebook) |
ISBN 9780231201124 (hardback) | ISBN 9780231201131
(trade paperback) | ISBN 9780231553940 (ebook)
Subjects: LCSH: State-sponsored terrorism—Spain—20th century. |
Violence—Spain—20th century. | Spain—Politics and
government—1939 -1975. | Human rights—Spain—20th century. |
Collective memory—Spain.
Classification: LCC HV6433.S7 I88 2022 (print) | LCC HV6433.S7
(ebook) | DDC 363.3250946—dc23
LC record available at https://lccn.loc.gov/2021034728
LC ebook record available at https://lccn.loc.gov/2021034729

Cover design: Noah Arlow
Cover image: AP Photo/Emilio Morenatti

—Para los sobrevivientes y luchadores contra el terrorismo del estado
—For my parents

ANTIGONE: Ismene, I am going to bury him. Will you come?

ISMENE: Bury him! You have just said the new law forbids it.

ANTIGONE: He is my brother. . . . And I will bury him; and if I must die, I shall lie down with him in death. . . . It is the dead, not the living, who make the longest demands: We die forever.

—Sophocles

CONTENTS

ACKNOWLEDGMENTS

This project began in 2013 while I was a graduate student at UCLA in desperate search of a dissertation project. I had long wanted to explore collective memories of the state violence in the southern cone but had been afraid of opening a Pandora's box of sorts. My Chilean father's life experiences had instilled in me a deep curiosity of the darkest side of humanity, as well as the continued impact of state terror. In the hope of further exploring these interests, I tentatively found myself first reading about Chile and then later about the Grandmothers of Plaza de Mayo in Argentina. I was compelled to further understand how their search for their missing grandchildren hinged so closely on their use and reification of genetic and forensic sciences. Next thing I knew I was in Argentina talking to the director of the Argentine Forensic Anthropology Team, Luis Fondebrider. From there, I found myself headed to Spain to further unpack the Argentine influence on a case that was substantially older (in terms of when the violence occurred), and at that time, less focused on academically. It was in Spain that I realized I had found not only my project but the story of my family retold in different iterations. It is not an understatement to say this experience changed the course of my life. Through it, I discovered my voice as a researcher, activist, and intellectual.

XII ℂ ACKNOWLEDGMENTS

I also lost, found, and recovered myself in the process. I will never have the right or enough words to explain the importance and meaning of this project and the people I met along the way. In the simplest terms, my deepest hope is that this book and the stories in it stay with you. May we learn from these violent pasts, so that they are not repeated in our futures.

This research would not have been possible without the generosity, support, and trust of the victims of violence and the human rights activists and scientists who fight alongside them. Their tireless commitment to truth and justice is an inspiration. I dedicate my work to you.

I am forever indebted to the team of the Association for the Recovery of Historical Memory, particularly Emilio, Marco, Nuria, Alex, René, Malena, Ruben, Cristina and Jesus, Laura, Juan Carlos, Ilhia, Amadeo, Iman, Ana, and Natalia. Thank you for allowing me to work alongside you in your important work. This book would not have been possible without you. Gracias Alex, René, Laura, Tserin (and your family) for all the beautiful memories of Bierzo. I also especially thank Oscar Rodriguez for his continued care and support. Thank you for sharing your photography with me and this book. Your images offer a voice that words cannot capture.

I would also like to thank the Grandmothers of the Plaza de Mayo, the International Committee on Missing Persons, the Committee for Missing Persons, the United Nations Working Group on Enforced and Involuntary Disappearance, and the Argentine Forensic Anthropology Team for sharing their stories and expertise with me.

Additionally, I thank my Madrid community, especially Carolina and Laura for your love and support. I also thank Penelope and Jax for the years of friendship and expat solidarity. I am so glad we met at that Hillary Clinton victory party. I can't wait for more adventures and eating divine foods.

As this project stems from my dissertation, I express my deepest gratitude to the UCLA College of Letters and Science Division of Social Sciences, the Department of Sociology, and the Latin American Institute for the financial support during the research years of this project. Furthermore, I would like to thank my dissertation committee: Gail Kligman, Abigail Saguy, Hannah Lendecker, and Geoffrey Robinson. To say I won the advisor lottery would not be an exaggeration. I thank all of you for your continued years of guidance and support. Gail, I will never be able to fully express the impact you have had on shaping my intellectual self or how grateful I am to have a life-long mentor like you. I look forward to many more years of listening to your brilliance and hoping some of it gleans onto me. I am also extremely grateful to Geoffrey Robinson for his mentorship and advising these many years. You are a true academic unicorn and inspiration. Thank you for your continued friendship and mentorship. I hope to carry forward your dedication to human rights advocacy and excellent scholarship throughout my life. I would also like to thank Aaron Panofsky who has so graciously taken me on as a mentee after graduate school. Thank you; I am forever indebted to you!

There are so many to thank at UCLA who were by my side during this project. I am extremely grateful to Rebecca DiBennardo, Ashley Gromis, Ariana Valle, Michael Stambolis (and Nick), Anne White, and Mirian Martinez-Aranda for their love, support, friendship, and never-ending encouragement. I am so lucky to have spent the last decade (plus) laughing, growing, and learning with you and from you. I would also like to thank Diya Bose, Karina Chavarria, Aaron Crawford, Juan Delgado, Leydy Diossa-Jimenez, Philippe Duhart, Zach Griffen, Jessica Huerta, Phi Hồng Sử, Rahim Kurwa, Shauna McManus, Saskia Nauenberg, Kevin Shih, Chris Rhea, Deisy Del Real, William Rosales,

Irene Vega, Sylvia Zamora, and Amy Zhou for all your support on this path.

This book would not exist if not for the support from Peter van der Veer and the Max Planck Institute for Religious and Ethnic Diversity, who provided the space, time, and financial support needed to develop the book into reality. I further thank the entire RDD department for their extremely helpful and constructive input on the various chapters of the book that they read. Living in Gottingen was challenging but was made a joyful and fulfilling experience due to the friends and colleagues at Max Planck. Thank you especially to Derek, Martjin, Leilah, Tim, Scott, Sabine, Jingyang, Vicky, Dora, and Jane for your love and friendship. I am so grateful our paths intersected.

Many others have provided valuable critiques, encouragement, and insights on this project. I have given many papers based on this book to the American Sociological Association, the Memory Studies Association, the Council on European Studies, the Young Scholars Conference at Notre Dame, the Social Problems Annual Meeting, the Radboud University of Nijmegen workshop on the Sociopolitical Life of Death, the Jean Monnet Centre Montreal's annual speaker series, and the Spanish National Research Council's Rastro y Rostros in Madrid. Members of these various audiences had thoughtful feedback and questions. I am especially grateful for feedback from Francisco Ferrándiz, Laura Martin-Chiappe, Tam Ngo, and Juliet Johnson and her seminar students. Additionally, I would like to express my deepest appreciation to my writing group. Thank you for reading so many iterations of this project and helping further develop and elevate it.

I thank my editors at Columbia University Press, Eric Schwartz and Lowell Frye, for believing in this project and helping make it a reality.

I would also like to thank the Huntington Beach Youth Shelter for having been my rock and other family since 2010. I would have lost my mind in graduate school and certainly wouldn't have been able to support my research trips if I hadn't worked at the shelter. I would especially like to thank my second mom, Elsa Greenfield, for her fierce support and love. Thank you, Amanda, Angie, Andy, Edgar, Jackie, John, Carlos, Carissa, Lauren, Matt, Nancy, Saida, and everyone I am inevitably forgetting. Thank you, front line workers, you are true heroes.

To my other loves, I appreciate your patience with my constant talk of state terror, enforced disappearance, and exhumations. I am particularly grateful to Brandy Roberts, Bridgette Amador, Elena Schionning, Mariah Cool, and Alexis Wolf for being by my side, in some cases, over half my life. You are my best friends and you have supported me through all the changes, joy, and pain. Thank you for being my sisters.

I would also like to thank my family for their love and support. Thank you, Jim Hecht, for being my big brother and being there for me in your way. You have always been my hero.

I remember looking at my mother's bound dissertation and saying, "you would have to be nuts to write a dissertation." I now know this to be unequivocally true and doubly so for a book. That said, I would like to thank both Dr. Rodolfo Iturriaga and Dr. Judith Iturriaga for their guidance, love, and never-ending and unyielding support, especially these last few years. I would not be here without it. I am who I am because of you, and I hope that I have made you proud.

And finally, to Jon, who came back into my life in a moment of global chaos, my childhood love. You—the kindest, brightest, most-fun-to-play-and-dance-with soul. Thank you for sharing love with me so fully and being exactly who you are. As Ram Dass would say, "We are all just walking each other home." Thank you for walking me home.

EXHUMING
VIOLENT
HISTORIES

INTRODUCTION

I n August 2015, I found myself working alongside the technical team of the Association for the Recovery of Historical Memory (ARMH) in the Andalusian heat to painstakingly uncover the mass grave of four victims of forced disappearance. The victims, two workers of the local village and their wives, had been brutally executed on a deserted road at the hands of rebel fighters in September 1936, two months after the beginning of the Spanish Civil War. The almost forty-year dictatorship that followed (1939–1975) mandated that victims like these be remembered only with disdain and disgust, as they were pronounced traitorous Marxists deserving of their deaths, their families denied the right to mourn or perform important death rites. The democratic transition (1975–1978) that followed the death of the dictator Francisco Franco also institutionalized a sanitized silence about the past, preserving the Francoist structure of victors and losers, all in the name of maintaining political stability. It wasn't until the new millennium that the global social movement of forensics-based human rights arrived in Spain and gave rise to Spanish human rights workers breaking both the repressive silence of the past and the ground to tell the true story of Spain's violent history.

Back at the grave, one of the women—Rosa—was revealed to have a red earring resting on her cranium; all four victims still had their wedding rings. Since this was my second exhumation ever, I was given the task of excavating—or removing the topsoil from—Rosa's feet, so that they would be completely uncovered. Due to the dryness of southern Spain, both the skeletal remains and the soles of the victims' shoes were well conserved (see fig. 0.1). As I was focusing on not breaking or ruining anything in the dig—in spite of the crash course training I received as an ARMH volunteer, ultimately, I am a sociologist, not an archeologist!—some locals from the village came by to see the work. They whispered that Rosa had been eight months pregnant at the time of her death. I kept working, all the while thinking about what they had said. Later, while uncovering her soles, it dawned on me that Rosa and I wore the same exact shoe size. I even held my shoe near hers to check. I then quickly scaled myself alongside her and discovered that we had the same build and stature. I was looking at myself in a mass grave.

The forensic analysis of Rosa's remains confirmed that she was around twenty to twenty-four years old at the time of death. She died, alongside her husband and his parents, from a bullet wound to the head and was buried facedown; what remained of her clothes was one red earring, a traditional Spanish hair comb, the soles of her shoes, and her wedding ring. As only one earring was found, it was thought she must have suffered some sort of violence where the other was knocked off. Small bone fragments thought to be fetal bones are still being analyzed by volunteer forensic anthropologists. In 2018, her village reburied her and the rest of the victims in a small ceremony. They honored them as the grandparents of democracy, who deserved to be buried and remembered with the deepest reverence.

FIGURE 0.1 The grave and victims' shoes with an ARMH team member

Exhuming Violent Histories is an ethnographic exploration of how social actors, like the ARMH described above, are using a variety of tools and tactics to fight for control over collective memories of state terror and to reconceptualize what obtaining justice for that terror means. Specifically, it looks at the global forensics-based human rights social movement through a case-study analysis of Spanish human rights workers and their use of both global and local tactics (performance, pedagogy, framing, transnational activist networks) to legitimize their movement's reframed narrative of Spain's past violence and achieve new forms of posttransitional justice. The book's central questions are focused on unpacking how human rights workers find authenticity through science, among other tactics, when engaging in memory wars over violent pasts: How do science and technology intersect human rights regimes and collective memory work, and how does this, in turn, impact justice models and efforts?

Succinctly, this book argues that human rights workers use forensic interventions—such as exhumations—to challenge dominant histories of violence, thereby contesting the state's control over historical memory. These workers, by grounding their claims in science, present themselves as credible and impartial rather than partisan and biased. In other words, they draw on science, international protocols, and tropes of modernity to depoliticize their account of state terror. As such, human rights workers, using what I call a "depoliticized approach," can meaningfully change dominant narratives of violence—such as how we remember the history of Rosa, her family, and why they were murdered—as well as shape new models of justice in cases of long-ago violence and continued impunity.

The Spanish case is unique because unlike other more famous cases of forensics-based human rights, such as in Argentina, Guatemala, or Bosnia and Herzegovina, the violence is not of the recent past. Most of the perpetrators and immediate survivors have already passed, with many grandchildren of the victims taking up the cause of finding their long-lost grandparents, or in some cases, great grandparents. Spain also stands apart because of how it transitioned to democracy in 1975. As will be further discussed in chapter 1, the centralized state reinforced a mandated and sanitized silence about the past during the democratic transition that lasted almost another forty years after the dictatorship ended. This silence maintained the Francoist structure that valorized the regime and brutally punished its victims at every turn.

However, in spite of these challenges and the lengthy period of time postviolence, Spanish civil society groups piggybacked off the developments in the Global South and in the world of forensics to challenge the repressive silence and the dominant collective memory of the past state terror. Their work has changed both the memory and the justice landscapes in Spain. Therefore, Spain represents an intriguing example of how global social movements and improvements in technology and forensic science can leapfrog to older cases of state-backed violence to revive and empower victims to fight for truth, justice, and memory.

Though the empirical research on these developments in Spain is substantial, this book adds to the larger scholarly conversation and demonstrates two innovative points.[1] First, the Spanish case is a clear example—and potential guide for other movements—of how expanding models of justice to include memory and forensic interventions by human rights and civil society groups can be both created and achieved in cases where it has been generationally elusive. Second, my analysis reveals the ways in which the Spanish case is an emblematic model for understanding how the larger global forensics-based human rights movement creates local variations that then adapt these tools to their cultural and social contexts. Meaning, through a case-study analysis of Spain, we can further unpack and illuminate larger processes of incorporation of global human rights ideas and tactics that evolve based on the needs of local cases. Further to this point, the book contributes to the literature by examining how ongoing actions of global human rights and international law can meaningfully impact the on-the-ground tactics, activities, and effect of local movements.

THEORIZING DEATH, JUSTICE, AND MEMORY

The story of this book, and forensics-based human rights in general, is at its core one of social actors seizing state necropower through a variety of tools such as science, framing, performativity, transnational networks, etc., to challenge how societies remember instances of state terror and create new models of justice. Necropower is the idea that governments threaten (or use) death to maintain control over their populations, including the historical narratives that explain the roles and importance of the dead for society (González-Ruibal and Ortiz García 2015; Mbembé 2003: 16; Robben 2015). Forensics-based human rights is a movement that attempts to commandeer power by literally uncovering and displaying bodies "disappeared" by the state.

It is important to note that within the processes of how societies construct their memories of the past, the role of the dead is particularly important. This applies to all dead citizens whether they are victims of state terror, dead soldiers, ex-state leaders, victims of a factory fire, etc., all of whom have agency and political lives. What I mean by that is that the dead are always potential symbolic political vehicles, open to social actors to create social and political reckonings (Gelonch-Solé 2013; Verdery 1999).

The dead, in addition to their political agency and lives, also have intrinsic self-worth, which demands respect from the living (Rubin 2016). German and Israeli courts have decreed that the dead are guaranteed certain legal rights, like the right to a decent burial (McCrudden 2008: 707–8). This idea is not particularly new or radical; Hugo Grotius argued in the fifteenth century that enemy soldiers deserved proper burials due to their basic human dignity (see also Grotius 2005: 1625; McCrudden 2008). The idea of respecting war dead has provided the foundation for the modern international legal order (McCrudden 2008; Rubin 2016). Even the ancient Greeks believed in the inherent rights of the dead, with many of their theatrical works making this claim, the most famous being *Antigone*. Thus, the dead can continue to make claims upon the state, long after they have died. Moreover, international law considers disappearance a crime against humanity, which has no statute of limitations, thus allowing victims of these crimes to potentially forever demand justice, making them even more powerful figures in society (Rosenblatt 2015).

However, as this book illustrates, in the Spanish case, human rights workers, through the use of forensic science, are resurrecting the long missing dead to challenge the longevity of Francoist necropower and the repressive silence that has lasted into the nascent democracy. Human rights workers, by exhibiting the tortured skeletons of the violent past, are loudly demanding recognition of the victims'—and their surviving families'—pain, and their long-denied humanity. Importantly, this research also demonstrates that the battles over dominant narratives of state violence are a significant iteration of obtaining a form of symbolic, yet somewhat tangible, justice.

Memory

Still, how we remember the past is complicated and should always be understood as "a layered field of sedimentation," whose strata are influenced by culture, emotions, storytelling, power relations, and the passing of time (Bodnar 1992; Gamson 2018; Marchart 2005: 25; Molden 2016). Collective memory also has many sources and actors who are making claims about the meaning of the past (Berger 2003: 7; Vinitsky-Seroussi 2002). Those holding privileged status in society, like state leaders, have greater opportunities and power to advance "official" accounts, as they monopolize the means of symbolic production (Bourdieu 1986; Whitlinger 2015: 650; Zerubavel 2006). For example, those in power control the systems of dispersion, such as the news media, have greater access to classified information, and speak the actual language of discussion. This can be especially true in societies that have suffered from political violence, war, or genocide (Ashplant, Dawson, and Roper 2000; Banjeglav 2013; Jelin 2003; Levy and Sznaider 2010). However, forensics-based human rights movements like the ARMH in Spain, for example, can create the political conditions for change and the opportunities for different understandings of justice that can be achieved in cases of countries with legal amnesty and long-ago state terror.

Nonetheless, the success of movements challenging collective memories depends on their perceived authenticity and legitimacy (Bourdieu 1986, 2004). Social movements that want to challenge how the past is remembered need to use "frames" that both authenticate their claims and resonate culturally with their target audiences (Armstrong and Crage 2006). By framing, I mean the process of using interpretive schemas, which individuals or groups use to negotiate, define, and understand their experiences within a social environment (Goffman 1974;

Oegema and Klandermans 1994; Snow et al. 1986). I argue throughout this book that forensics-based human rights workers have been able to achieve resonance, authenticity, and legitimacy through the use of two master frames: the rights of families and depoliticized science. A "master frame" is a way of understanding the world in an elastic enough way that a wide range of social movements can adopt it (Snow and Benford 1988).

The rights of families frame derives from a sizable sociological and anthropological literature, which argues that the death of a human being provokes culturally universal social and moral obligations conveyed through specified funerary practices (Hertz 2017; Robben 2017). When a state kills someone and makes their body impossible to find—or disappears them, like Rosa and her family—those individuals are denied all funerary rites and no longer have their individual or collective identity (Gelonch-Solé 2013; ICPPED 2006; Robben 2017). States that use disappearances, arbitrary executions, and unmarked graves do it to sow terror and repress resistance to their power. It is also a form of emotional torture, as one ARMH worker explained: "It's the not knowing, the absence. It is like a double death." Therefore, ARMH members using the "rights of families" frame focus on the need for both clarifying the truth about past violence *and* the rights of the families to understand the fate of their loved ones (including those who may still be alive), as opposed to emphasizing the politics of the violence.

The depoliticized science frame, alternatively, stems from cultural beliefs about public trust in science and its perceived objectivity. The trustworthiness of scientific knowledge is connected to cultural understandings about its political objectivity and neutrality, which are vital for building social harmonies (Gauchat 2012: 168). Nikolas Luhmann (1979) contends that public trust in science is a form of faith in the specialized knowledge that guides our perceptions of complex problems of the world, like fighting disease. Yet, in recent decades, there has been a noted decrease in the public's trust in science, or belief that scientific outcomes reflect political ideologies, specifically about climate change, COVID-19, and vaccines (Gauchat 2012; Lewandowsky and Oberauer 2016). This distrust maybe reflects "the negative consequences of industrialization, technocratic authority" and the loosening of the cultural authority of science (Beck 1992: 156; for more on this see Camargo Jr and Grant 2015; Hamilton, Hartter, and Saito 2015; Makarovs and Achterberg 2018).

In spite of this concerning shift in the public's belief in the validity of science, in the case of human rights, forensic science remains an invaluable tool (Rosenblatt 2015; Sanford 2003). Previous scholarly work has consistently demonstrated that the public accepts forensic science as being objective, untainted by politics, and therefore an arbiter of truth (Donnelly 2012: 94; Schweitzer and Saks 2007; Specht 2013). The scholarship on forensics-based human rights activism has also illustrated that, in the majority of cases, once human rights workers provide scientific evidence, such as DNA identifications of bodies in mass graves with 99.9 percent accuracy, it can be difficult for rivals to reasonably contend that the human rights workers' version of violent pasts are false or corrupted by politics (Rosenblatt 2015; Sanford 2003).

The depoliticized science frame thus works to simplify and condense the human rights workers' counter-memory of state terror as being merely the result of objective scientific findings from exhumations, DNA identifications, and historical research, as opposed to political motivation or malice. Of course, the success of this frame depends on the national, cultural, and political situations of each case (see Rosenblatt 2015; Sanford 2003; Wagner 2008). Indeed, there is great potential for tension between human rights and science in epistemological and justice projects such as

the Grandmothers of Plaza de Mayo's reification of genetic identity (Gandsman 2009b, 2009a; Iturriaga 2019); the complicated
Bosnian case where underlying and historical tensions have been
used to discredit or ignore forensic findings (see Wagner 2008 for
a brilliantly nuanced analysis of the Bosnian case and its difficulties); or cases of misidentification in Argentina, Chile, Bosnia,
and Cyprus (for more on this see Rosenblatt 2015).

To be clear, this book understands the term *depoliticized* to refer
to science's *perceived* objectivity in its findings, which allows it to
be seen as incorruptible and free from political manipulation (for
a deeper understanding of de/politicization see Cech and Sherick
2015; Maeseele et al. 2017; Pepermans and Maeseele 2014). I am
not conceptualizing these frames as being apolitical. Rather, apolitical framing efforts are often inherently political in that human
rights workers are engaging in overtly political acts with explicit
political goals using depoliticized techniques and strategies. I am
also suggesting that due to the authenticity that these frames
provide, new forms of justice (breaking silences, exhuming, identifying, reburying victims, and challenging/rewriting narratives of
violence) become more palatable and achievable.

In sum, these two frames draw on preexisting and resonant
cultural beliefs around the moral importance of familial obligations and the perceived legitimacy and objectivity of science,
which human rights workers use to make claims about past violence and present new conceptions and forms of justice, especially useful in cases of long-ago violence or where barriers to
legal justice exist.

(Post)Justice

What does justice mean in the case of Spain? Traditionally,
transitional justice is understood to be measures seen to reform,

reunite, and stabilize a conflict-torn society and reestablish peace, the rule of law, security, and democracy (Banjeglav 2013; Mihr 2017). As will be discussed more deeply in chapter 1, Spain, after Franco's death in 1975, went through what is known as a negotiated transition (1975–1978), which ultimately maintained key governmental structures and leaders, such as judges and governmental power brokers from the dictatorship. Moreover, the political elite also passed a blanket amnesty law that still exists and is enforced. During this time period, academic and diplomatic ideas about truth and reconciliation were not commonly used for democratic transitions; this became more normalized in the late 1980s and early 1990s. Spain never engaged with truth and reconciliation efforts even after they became popularized.

It should be noted that Spanish victims of state terror and their families have never had access to criminal justice options due to the amnesty law. Moreover, many victims' families have tried to get around these restrictions by taking their cases to the European Court of Human Rights and other global courts but have been repeatedly denied (Ryan 2017; Ugarte 2017). Due to the amount of time since the transition, Spanish civil society groups such as the ARMH are engaging in what some scholars call "posttransitional justice" (Aguilar 2008; Golob 2008; Kovras 2013; Raimundo 2012). These efforts are happening in spite of the state's intentions, as it has largely been obstinate to any and all justice efforts.

This book adds to the larger and more nuanced conversations about democratic transitions to more fully include and incorporate the role of transnational influences, such as global forensics-based human rights and transnational legal advocacy networks within these multilayered posttransitional justice efforts. Furthermore, Spain, as a case-study example of the transnational impact and evolution of global movements, can also be understood as a potential model or guide for cases of long-ago state violence and terror, such as Indonesia or the United States such as the recent exhuming of bodies in Tulsa, Oklahoma, from the Black Wall Street massacre of 1921.

FORENSIC SCIENCE: ARBITER OF TRUTH

Spanish human rights workers have been able to make these posttransitional gains due to the global forensics-based human rights movement, which leapfrogged to Spain in the year 2000. The now global forensics-based human rights movement actually first began in postauthoritarian Argentina in the mid-1980s, when forensic anthropology intersected human rights and democratic transition politics.[2] This intersection sparked a small revolution in global human rights regimes and began a powerful transnational social movement, which has been described by some as the "forensic turn" while others call it a "forensics cascade" (Colaert 2016; Dziuban 2017; Kovras 2017).[3]

By the end of Argentina's last military dictatorship (1976–1983), over thirty thousand people were "disappeared," alongside their five hundred living children, many born in clandestine prisons and then adopted by members of the regime under false identities. (For more on the Dirty War see Bouvard 2002; Feitlowitz 2011; Robben 2000; Smith 2016.)[4] Victims' families organizations, notably the Mothers and Grandmothers of Plaza de Mayo, organized demanding information on the whereabouts of their missing family members. (For more on these groups, including gendered analysis, see Bosco 2004; Bouvard 2002; Burchianti 2004; Jelin and Kaufman 2017; Pauchulo 2009; Rosenblatt 2015.) Their activism, along with transnational partnerships, led to both the downfall of the regime and the rise of the global movement of forensics-based human rights (Arditti 2002; Bouvard 2002; Rosenblatt 2015).

After the regime fell, the transitional government invited international experts, at the behest of the Mothers and Grandmothers of Plaza de Mayo, including Clyde Snow, a forensic anthropologist, to help in the transition. Snow, in 1986, established the nongovernmental Argentine Forensic Anthropology Team—known by its Spanish acronym, EAAF—and trained them in the forensic techniques for locating, exhuming, and identifying the missing (Moon 2013). It was during these exhumations that Snow and the fledgling EAAF found forensic evidence that some of the female prisoners had given birth before their executions (Joyce and Stover 1991).[5] As there were no signs of fetal or baby remains, this strongly suggested that the children had been taken alive. This event spurred the second arm of the forensics-based human rights movement that focuses on the use of genomic blood testing to identify both the living and dead disappeared (Arditti 2002; Gandsman 2009b; Iturriaga 2019). In Argentina, the success of blood testing to prove the existence of stolen children, alongside the forensic work of the EAAF, unequivocally changed the memory landscape of how the violence of the regime was understood by both the state and society. It also marked the first time *ever* that activists had used forensic science to refute and renarrate a collective memory of state terror (Rosenblatt 2015).[6]

The EAAF—simultaneously and alongside the Grandmothers—went on to be one of the most important innovators and diffusers of forensic anthropological practices in global human rights (Crossland 2013; Kovras 2017; Moon 2013: 154). They did this initially through their south-south approach, meaning teaching others in the Global South their techniques and protocols so they would not have to rely on the Global North or regional governmental agencies with proven records of corruption or violence. By the mid-1990s, the EAAF had worked in almost forty countries, had participated in more than ten truth commissions including ones in El Salvador, Guatemala, Iraq, Kurdistan, and Ethiopia, and had taken part in trials of human rights abusers as expert witnesses (Bernardi and Fondebrider 2007; Blau and Skinner 2005; Crossland 2013: 129; Drawdy and Katzmarzyk 2016; Fondebrider 2002; Joyce and Stover 1991; Kovras 2017). Importantly, the EAAF also directly facilitated setting up forensic teams in, among other countries, Guatemala (FAFG, Forensic Anthropology Foundation of Guatemala), Cyprus (CMP, Committee on Missing Persons), and Peru (EPAF, Peruvian Team of Forensic Anthropology) (Juhl 2005; Kovras 2017). Since 2015, the EAAF has worked alongside and directly supported the Spanish ARMH by facilitating all of their DNA testing needs.

As forensics-based human rights has grown, so has the field. The principal disciplines making up forensic science are forensic archeology, anthropology, and pathology. Forensic archeology applies and draws on the traditional principles and methodologies of archeology to find graves and exhume them, while ensuring the preservation of bodies, objects, and evidence (Obledo 2009; Rosenblatt 2015).[7] Archeologists are also trained in identifying skeletal features, creating sizable overlap with forensic anthropologists. Forensic anthropologists, however, specialize in the human osteology, the study of skeletal remains, as well as physical or biological anthropology. Forensic anthropologists can articulate, or assemble in order, skeletons, analyze their biological profiles, meaning their stature, sex, age, and ancestry, as well as recognize signs of disease or physical trauma. The difference between the two fields often relates to the educational opportunities and approaches in particular countries (Rosenblatt 2015).

Like any science, forensic science has protocols designed to ensure the work is conducted in a methodologically consistent way. These protocols cover exhumations and autopsy procedures, among a myriad of other concerns.[8] Yet within forensics-based human rights protocols there are two clear distinctions between "humanitarian" and judicial.[9] The basic difference is that humanitarian protocols are focused explicitly on working with victims' families and with the clear objective of identifying the remains, so they can be reburied according to the family's wishes, whereas judicial interventions are focused on proving a crime against humanity took place.

Yet, across my fifty-five interviews with technicians and forensics experts, many argued that humanitarian efforts and legal justice are two sides of the same coin (Congram and Sterenberg 2009: 447–48; Fondebrider 2002). For example, humanitarian forensics protocols also record evidence in ways that could be used in future legal prosecutions. For example, if an amnesty law is revoked, the evidence from graves could be used in court to prove crimes against humanity (Crossland 2013). Furthermore, across my interviews, many contended that their work also provides incontrovertible truth about these crimes and sets "the historical record straight" (Kirschner and Hannibal 1994: 453). The idea here is that the scientific evidence and findings help to construct new understandings of the history that have been hidden or twisted by brutal regimes (Doretti and Snow 2003: 293). My interviewees, across the board, argued that science can correct the historical record from denial and revision, especially since the forensic reports created by these interventions are historical records, which are more difficult to deny (Doretti and Snow 2003: 293).

Additionally, like with the ARMH, among other teams around the world, nonexperts also work alongside professional technicians, developing a certain level of expertise in the field of forensics-based human rights. The ARMH trains many of its volunteers in the basics of forensic archeology and has them work alongside the experts of the team. This is mostly due to the need for extra hands in the exhumation process, which is faster with more people. Steve Epstein (1996) calls this "expertification," meaning that laypersons have gained a certain level of "expertise" in their particular fields. Expertification complicates how scholars evaluate the expression of expertise, as well as its impact on social behavior and consequences, especially in human rights, social justice, and health policies. I argue, in line with Gil Eyal (2013), that the conceptualization of expertise should be inclusive enough to encompass other actors who may have achieved expert level knowledge on a topic. Additionally, I posit that in the case-study example of Spanish forensics-based human rights, what is most important is the public's belief that the ARMH has expert knowledge. This project treats all individuals who participate in this organization as experts, regardless of their academic background, status, or profession (Stambolis-Ruhstorfer 2015). However, there is a still of spectrum of expertise within the organization with technical experts running the technical work. This understanding of expertise is useful in that it allows for the analysis of the conditions and mechanisms, such as transitional networks or international treaties, which influence the construction of knowledge without having to make assumptions about what counts as expertise.

Forensics-based human rights teams thus include a wide variety of actors and use many scientific methodologies and technologies to assist in the investigation of human rights violations (Burns 1999: 205). Therefore, these human rights workers using "technologies of truth" have in a little over thirty years become vital instruments of transitional justice (Kovras 2017).

The transnational forensics-based human rights movement, and the technologies it employs, have facilitated thousands of families to recover and identify their missing (Ferllini 2007; Haglund, Connor, and Scott 2001).[10]

WHY DO WE TRUST FORENSIC SCIENCE?

Societal trust in forensic science is both intriguing and important for understanding the work and power of forensics-based human rights movements, like the ARMH. To unpack this, I look to the broad field of Science and Technology Studies (STS), which seeks to understand the ways that scientific knowledge becomes rooted in social structures, institutions, representations, identities, and discourses (Lawless 2016: 2). STS thus offers a useful framework for understanding everyday practices, such as those examined in this book, which produce scientific knowledge and its effects (Kruse 2015: 10). Previous STS research on forensic science has examined its relationship to the law (Lynch and McNally 2003), legal decision-making (Lynch 2013), legal outcomes (Cole 2009; Lynch 2013; Lynch and Cole 2005), as well as forensic science's relationship citizenship (Lawless 2013; Lynch and Jasanoff 1998), and state power (Toom, Hindmash, and Prainsack 2010). Building off the extant STS literature, I suggest that this trust in forensics is due to four concurring phenomena: 1) society and scientists have "co-produced" forensic science; 2) forensics-based human rights workers use distancing tactics to protect themselves from being perceived as politically biased; 3) forensic science is accessible and easy to understand; and 4) forensic science reflects societal morals that we theoretically believe in.[11]

One of the reasons I argue we believe forensic science is that we have cocreated it with scientists. But what does that entail?

Bruno Latour (1987) and Shelia Jasanoff (2004) have both argued that scientific knowledge is created by society and scientists together. The merging of knowledge—as opposed to empirical realities or findings—is what gives scientific claims their social stability (Oreskes 2019: 70). Therefore, scientific thought should be considered part of our collective conscious. Moreover, scientific outcomes are converted into knowledge due to the processes of critical reception (Oreskes 2019).

How then do forensics-based human rights and depoliticized framing fit into the collective conscious and cocreation of science? First, it is the science of the state. For example, forensic science is what police and prosecutors use to bring individuals to a court of law to face legal justice. This science includes fingerprints, DNA samples, gun residue, etc. In many ways, human rights workers' use of forensic science is somewhat ironic, as it has been used to hold rogue states accountable for violent actions (sometimes superseding the state's sovereignty) and by states to persecute citizens. It is also the science of police shows. These shows have created what some have called "The CSI Effect," or the idea that forensic science is "infallible—100 percent reliable, with no margin for doubt" (Carracedo and Prieto 2019), which also illustrates forensic science's elasticity and perceived impartiality across multiple fields.

Interestingly, scholarly work on the CSI Effect has shown that jurors are more likely to side with the prosecution when there is forensic evidence. However, the impact of CSI is not relegated solely to courtrooms; it has also lent legitimacy to forensics-based human rights all the way up to the international level. In a 2015 interview with Ariel Dulitzky, the director of the United Nations Working Group on Enforced or Involuntary Disappearances, he said, "[Forensics] is vital. Without it, you can't prove anything. Everyone should have it, or they should have the international community providing access to it." For my interlocutors CSI also emerged as a focus point. For some it was a good thing. One forensic anthropologist, Kostas, working in Cyprus posited, "In recent years, there have been many TV programs showing how DNA has affected how we find people.[12] And because all of this, now people believe DNA. To me, CSI is a little bit, maybe not 100 percent correct, but some things are true . . . most importantly it shows that you can, and should, believe in DNA." As such, CSI, though potentially problematic, has helped to both introduce forensic science concepts and ideas to worldwide audiences and cement its legitimacy and authority.

Another reason we trust forensic science has to do with distancing. The EAAF, among many other forensics-based human rights teams, go out of their way to separate their technicians from those who make political statements. Through the cultural sociology literature, we know that people draw boundaries, likening themselves to others and comparing their situations, creating exclusive boundaries, and by positioning themselves as different from others (Lamont 1992; Lamont and Molnár 2002). In this case, distancing is being used to separate the technical teams and their outcomes from political claims. Teams like the International Committee on Missing Persons (ICMP) in Bosnia and Herzegovina, the Committee on Missing Persons (CMP) in Cyprus, etc., all differentiate parts of their teams that are either strictly technical or involved in the public domain. It is the same for the ARMH, which is split into one group that does the technical work while the other deals with public relations and makes moral, political, or judicial claims.

Depoliticized scientific framing can thus be seen as a form of distancing to protect the scientists/activists from the political implications of the scientific outcomes. Throughout my fifty-five interviews with global forensics-based human rights experts working across the world, the majority denied that they were activists. However, most also took on the mantle and language of human rights when discussing the impact and function of science in human rights interventions, such as ensuring historical records were accurate. Luis Fondebrinder, the current director of the EAAF, perhaps put this stance most clearly when he said he was a "scientist compromised with the realities of human rights." The scientists in forensics-based human rights are humans working to prove the worst of humanity's possibilities. It seems inevitable that this would affect how they view what they are doing. One could argue that scientists focused on ending diseases or social ills like starvation may similarly believe that their work can better society without necessarily describing themselves as activists. Intrinsically, the biggest takeaway in the world of forensics-based human rights and why the public believes the science to be objective is framing resonance, or how people understand the frame (Benford and Snow 2000; Snow and Benford 1988; Whitlinger 2015). Resonance is so important that previous scholarship has shown that if a frame is resonant with a target audience, it will be effective even if it is demonstrably false (Benford and Snow 2000; Fine 1995; Kolker 2004).

Yet, perhaps one of the more compelling mechanisms explaining why we trust forensic science is accessibility. Forensic science, unlike complex ideas like climate change or even vaccines, is easily understood on one level. Unlike other forms of science, or even the actual science used in forensics such as DNA testing, it is not necessary for nonprofessionals, especially outside of juries, to understand the mechanisms that create the scientific outcomes. They just need to understand the conclusions. Human remains with clear signs of violence, such as bullet wounds, ligatures, or torture-induced fractures, are extremely powerful evidence, due to their ability to "speak" a clear truth. One does not need to have gone to university or have an advanced degree, or even be an adult, to understand what a bullet through the head signifies. To put it in positivist science terms, the simplicity of some forensic outcomes relies heavily on verification; someone shot this other person in the head and then they died.

And finally—if all of these mechanisms weren't enough—forensic science, in the field of human rights, may also be deemed more legitimate because it reflects our moral values, such as the value of human life and the importance of objective truth. Some scholars (Oreskes 2019; Oreskes and Conway 2011; Webb and Hayhoe 2017) have suggested that when science reflects people's values, they are more likely to believe it. For example, Naomi Oreskes has demonstrated that many people disregard climate science not because the science is wrong but rather because it conflicts, or is perceived to conflict, with their personal values, economic interests, or political ideologies (2019: 147). Trust in science is easier to establish when the values are shared. I argue that this is one of the key reasons that the application of forensic science in the realm of human rights has been so successful; it reflects larger societal values that we theoretically believe in.

Human rights, or the idea that all human beings have fundamental dignity and worth, is something that has been continually reaffirmed and shared. A version of this is found in the three major world religions—which encompass almost four billion people—all three concurring that we should not steal, commit adultery, bear false witness, or kill (Oreskes 2019: 159). Human rights norms have also become profoundly institutionalized in both domestic and international law and institutions, including in the developing world (Sikkink 2019). Though international human rights are not a perfect enterprise, they have made a powerful and indelible impact due to their reflection of these larger societal goals and values.

In sum, I argue that forensics-based human rights arguments and findings are more readily believed than other forms of science—in combination with the other cited mechanisms—because forensics-based human rights reflect back our larger values, which are shared with the scientists and technicians who are doing this work. These shared beliefs in human rights and justice help make the claims and findings both more believable and resonant. For most, the findings of forensics-based human rights do not threaten or contradict peoples' values or their way of life. Rather, they reflect our theoretical belief in the dignity and worthiness of human life, our concepts of truth-informing fairness, and our goals of achieving innovative models of justice for victims and their families.

CASE STUDY

This book thus approaches these broad and intersecting ideas and topics through an in-depth ethnographic case study of Spain's most famous human rights forensic organization, the ARMH. I selected the ARMH because it was the originator of the historical memory movement, the first to introduce forensics-based human rights to Spain, and because at the time I was conducting fieldwork, it was one of the most active and recognized organizations doing exhumations in Spain.

The ARMH is also an ideal organization to evaluate social actors using the depoliticized science approach to seize control over historical memories of state terror. Other organizations that mobilized in Spain in the early 2000s, like Forum for Memory—which also engaged in scientific exhumations and was at times a vocal critic of the ARMH's depoliticized approach (Bevernage and Colaert 2014; Ferrándiz 2013; Rubin 2018)—aggressively put forward leftist political arguments and sentiments, and displayed political symbols during technical work. Additionally, Forum for Memory was affiliated with, and included, political parties, like the Communist Party, in their exhumation work. However, over time it was unable to sustain its exhumation efforts and has since switched focus toward online educational and protest events. It has also been vocal in supporting the exhumation of those buried at the Valley of the Fallen. That the ARMH, however, continues to perform exhumations, hold memory events, and have a formidable voice in the memory politics of Spain, which this book illustrates, is due in large part to its effective navigation of the political terrain by framing its work around depoliticized science and the rights of victims' families.

Another important aspect to the ARMH's navigation of the political landscape is also reflected in how it categorizes members into different groupings. For example, as previously mentioned, it distinguishes among technical workers, activists (the public side, such as the president, Emilio Silva), and volunteers. These distinctions also reveal a depoliticized approach, as the technical workers are separated, theoretically, from those making political arguments. As we will see later, the reality is much more complicated, as technical workers often put forth scientific findings alongside political, moral, and justice-based claims.

The ARMH also has ongoing working collaborations with important human rights groups in Argentina, among other transnational actors, making this a particularly compelling case to analyze how transnational networks and the diffusion of forensic science can lead to the demand and achievement of some new forms of justice. Due to these networks, the Spanish case provides an opportunity for the comprehensive exploration of the on-the-ground effects that transnational human rights advocacy, networks, and forensics-based human rights can have on a postauthoritarian state that has refused to confront its past. My aim here is to elucidate how the science and technology of forensics intersect the reframing of collective memories of violence and state terror and how it is used to break down repressive silencing of the past, reconstruct how Spain remembers its violent history, and expand our conceptions and means for justice in long-ago cases of state terror.

The data for this book draws on fifteen months of participant observations conducted across two waves: one in 2015 and another in 2016 and 2017 with the ARMH. During my time in the field, I did two hundred informal interviews with nonactivist Spaniards who were either in attendance at mass grave exhumations or other memory events; fifteen formal interviews with human rights workers and fifteen non-activists; and a content analysis of exhumation guest books and a content analysis of local media coverage of a homage and reburial ceremony. Together, I use this data to analyze the various mechanisms (performance, pedagogy, globalized conceptions of human rights, transnational advocacy networks, and international law) that ARMH workers use to further their goals of exposing the truth of the past, as well as restoring memory, identity, and justice within a globalized context. Though the book predominately relies on the ethnography and qualitative interviews in Spain, I also pull supplementary data from research conducted in Argentina, as well as an additional fifty-five interviews with technicians and experts working in forensics-based human rights teams and organizations across the world. (Please see the methodological appendix for a more in-depth review of my methodologies and discussions on positionality and reflexivity.) Like any study, this research has its limitations including that most of the fieldwork was conducted in the northwest region of the country, the informal interviews were comprised of a mostly convenience sample of individuals who walked up to technical fieldwork sites, and it focuses only on the work of the ARMH, as opposed to a comparison of other civil society organizations. Notwithstanding, the data still provides rich opportunities to unpack the work of the ARMH, how it has impacted both victims' families and local communities, and how its work is emblematic of new visions and models of post-transitional justice in cases of long-ago violence, legal amnesty, and general disinterest of the centralized state.

CHAPTER OVERVIEW

This introduction has offered a concise review of the rise of the forensics-based human rights social movement and the guiding theoretical frameworks and larger arguments of the book. Throughout *Exhuming Histories*, I demonstrate how forensics-based human rights workers are using a variety of mechanisms, including framing their work around the rights of families and depoliticized science, to seize control of historical narratives of state violence and terror, while also creating and actualizing new forms of justice.

Chapter 1, "No Pasarán? The Spanish Civil War, the Franco Regime, and Democracy," lays the historical groundwork of the Spanish case. It begins by briefly reviewing what led to the Spanish Civil War, the violence of the war, the Franco regime (1939–1975) and how it maintained control through fear and repression, and the democratic transition (1975–1978). This chapter also covers how the Franco regime maintained a terrorized silence about its past violence and how many Spaniards complied with the regime to survive its repression. The democratic transition continued this sanitized silence under the guise that it protected Spain from political instability. Consequently, many

Spaniards, even today, mostly in rural areas, find disrupting this silence to be frightening.

This chapter then more closely examines how changing international human rights ideals led to the development of the Spanish ARMH in 2000 and the incorporation of forensics-based human rights in Spain. It also highlights the Spanish case's ongoing overlap and connection with Argentina.

Chapter 2, "Excavations: A Scientific Trojan Horse," explores how the ARMH breaks the repressive silence of the past through performative social actions that ground its work in science and community collaboration, which I argue is an actualized form of justice. Chapter 2 begins by examining how scientific excavations of mass graves act as the beginning of many social interactions between the ARMH and villagers. I demonstrate how the physical space of the technical work facilitates interactions and performative acts, like storytelling, that effectively break the silence. I then analyze how the ARMH incorporates collaborative community work, as well as how the ARMH deals with hostile interactions. Next, I illustrate that throughout these interactions, even the hostile ones, human rights workers are actualizing the social change they seek to create, breaking the repressive silence of the past, introducing reframed narratives of the violence, and destigmatizing the long-suffering victims and their families, an important model of posttransitional justice. Additionally, chapter 2 illuminates how ARMH technical interventions give human rights workers the chance to introduce their grounding movement frames, specifically the rights of the families to bury their dead and the power-of-science approach that bases their work in depoliticized science.

Chapter 3, "At the Foot of the Grave: Teaching Science and the 'True' History of Spain," analyzes the ARMH's pedagogical actions, the "history and forensics classes" that the ARMH offers to locals visiting mass grave exhumations. The chapter demonstrates how the ARMH uses pedagogy to introduce a reframed historical account of the violence through the lens of forensic science. This tactic is a powerful tool because it continues to rupture the repressive silence, reframes the victims as actual victims of unjustified state terror rather than as communists deserving of violent deaths, illuminates the failures of the democratic transition, and—like other forms of testimony—places the responsibility for seeking justice on the witnesses who are listening to the classes. Moreover, using this tactic, ARMH technical workers present themselves as legitimate practitioners of knowledge—telling the stories of and from the graves through science and modernism, even though their message is inherently political. They also let both the bodies and found personal objects "speak" their truths, which works to bolster the technicians' legitimacy and reframing of the past. Chapter 3 also illustrates how the scientific forward approach creates the space for the technicians to introduce political ideas about transitional justice and memory politics.

Chapter 4, "Reburying the Dead: Performance of Grief and Reframed Narratives," explores the more theatrical and performative tactics of the ARMH, specifically the homage and reburial ceremonies for the recovered dead. The chapter argues that homage and reburial ceremonies put on by the ARMH force local Spanish communities and the larger society to view the consequences of the past violence, which is still "present in the lived experience" of the victims' families. The chapter thus clarifies how these events also offer families the opportunity to bury their dead according to their religious and cultural beliefs and allow them to express public grief, and potentially the chance to obtain closure, an important kind of posttransitional justice. Moreover, it evaluates how these events encourage more performative public storytelling and historical descriptions of the violence, often backed by the ARMH's forensic evidence.

Furthermore, this chapter demonstrates how reburial and homage ceremonies offer an interesting perspective; not only do these delayed death rites create a public space to grieve and mourn, but they are also an avenue to critique established power, such as the state. It also illustrates how public homage and reburial ceremonies can provide a form of truth and reconciliation at the local village level that has never occurred in Spain. This section additionally includes a content analysis of local news media coverage of one of the case study's reburial and homage events to analyze the meso-level impact of these events.

Chapter 5, "Transnational Networks," investigates the ARMH's international connections and their impact on the movement and its goals of reframing the dominant narrative of violence in Spain. The chapter focuses on the exceptional nature of the exhumations in Guadalajara, Spain, as they were a direct result of the Argentinean-led universal jurisdiction case investigating Franco-era crimes against humanity. Chapter 5 accordingly illustrates the intersecting mechanisms at work during the exhumations that then allow transnational influences to be incorporated into already existing ARMH movement tactics, which help further implement a new understanding of justice at the micro, meso, and macro levels. Moreover, the chapter explores the distinctive consequences created by these transnational relationships between the ARMH and the international community.

1

NO PASARÁN? THE SPANISH CIVIL WAR, THE FRANCO REGIME, AND DEMOCRACY

The Spanish Civil War

The world in the 1930s was chaotic. In Spain, underlying social and political instability was further exacerbated by the Great Depression, which led to mass job loss, strikes, political violence, inflation, homelessness, and hunger. In other parts of Western Europe, economic misery was fueling the rise of a dangerous strain of right-wing nationalism that led to violent purges of both political rivals and local scapegoats. For example, in 1934, Adolf Hitler solidified his power when his supporters gunned down his rivals in the Night of the Long Knives. That same year also saw Italy's dictator, Benito Mussolini, similarly terrorize and purge any resistance to his rule (Hochschild 2016; Preston 2012).

However, in February 1936, Spain bucked the fascist trend by voting in the Popular Front, an alliance made up of leftist, communist, and socialist parties that narrowly defeated right-wing challengers who were heavily backed by wealthy industrialists, landowners, and the Catholic Church. For a country that still lagged behind the majority of Western Europe, this was an unexpected democratic triumph. The new government of the Second Republic, the name of the Spanish democracy, promised rapid and far-reaching changes including decreasing the military's budget to provide programs for the poor. Yet, stock markets fell as leftists and peasants occupied both factories and large estates, while others jubilantly burned churches (Hochschild 2016; Preston 2012). The Catholic Church was supportive and loyal to the power elite and were thus subjected to violence by those who felt oppressed by the church's conservative politics.

Spain up until this time had a long history of military coups d'états and political instability; thus, the new leadership of the Second Republic, in an attempt to learn from history, assigned right-wing generals to faraway posts. The government sent one such general, Francisco Franco, who had successfully suppressed a miners' revolt in 1934, to the Canary Islands, while others went to Morocco and other Spanish outposts in Africa. Unfortunately for the Second Republic, these faraway positions allowed conspirators to plan an overthrow without suspicion.

The Coup d'état of 1936

In spite of the Second Republic's best efforts to prevent a governmental overthrow, right-wing generals began planning their rebellion immediately. They organized their uprising to be executed with a "scorched-earth ferocity" that had rarely been seen inside of Europe since the Middle Ages and was often saved for colonial takeovers (Graham 2005; Hochschild 2016: 26). The rebelling military used the code word "Covadonga," referring to a key eighth-century battle in the fight to "recover" Spain from Muslim rule. The generals used this word because they believed that the Second Republic, like the Muslims of an earlier century, represented a dangerous and foreign enemy, from which Spain needed protection at all costs. Democracy, for the cabal of generals leading the revolt, was extremely threatening, as they were convinced that democracy would lead to a Spanish version of the Russian Revolution. Those participating in the uprising thus called themselves "Nacionales," which according to historian Paul Preston, connotes the idea of "only true Spaniards," rather than how it translates into English as "the nationalists" (Hochschild 2016: 26; Preston 2007: 26). I, however, will be referring to the revolting military as either "rebels" or "Francoists," depending on whether it was before or after October 1, 1936, when Franco became leader of the coup, as it is more historically accurate to their positions in the war. Additionally, using the word *nationalists* erases the historical fact that there were nationalist fighters on both sides of the war, including Catalan and Basque nationalists who fought on the Republican side.

The generals strategically used their exiled positions in Spanish Africa and surrounding colonies to recruit additional fighters. In Morocco, for example, the generals enlisted Arab fighters for the rebellion through manipulation, telling them that they were waging war against those who wanted to destroy Islam. Through such a lie, the generals amassed forty thousand experienced troops waiting to enter Spain at their command. Those in the army who remained loyal to the democracy were shot, including seven generals and an admiral.

General Francisco Franco, though not originally the leader of the revolt, soon began to take charge. Franco was the "army's most competent general . . . [He was] ambitious and puritanical, an architect of the elite Spanish Foreign Legion . . . driven by a fierce belief that he was destined to save Spain from a deadly conspiracy of Bolsheviks, Freemasons, and Jews" (Hochschild 2016: 26). As the air force and navy stayed loyal to the Republic, Franco went to Mussolini and Hitler for support. They happily obliged by sending troops, weapons, and naval and air support,

which helped the rebels to gain and maintain military suprem-
acy from the start of the conflict. In the civil war that followed,
Hitler tested twenty-seven different models of Nazi aircraft and
aviation maneuvers long before he used them in global conflict.

On July 17, 1936, the Spanish Civil War began. Hundreds
of army officers commanding tens of thousands of troops took
control of Spanish Morocco[1], the surrounding areas, and Spanish islands. The rebels, with support from their fascist allies,
transported loyal troops onto mainland Spain, invading from
the Moroccan southern entry point. The leaders' intent was for
all military posts to rise up throughout the country, ensuring a
swift takeover of the government. As soon as the army sent the
word, officers across Spain rounded up any officials, and later,
any supporters, of the Second Republic. Parts of Spain, such
as the northwest Galician region, fell immediately, while other
parts held off the coup through fierce fighting. The first several
months of combat created an oddly shaped Spain; the Republic maintained control of Spain's three largest cities—Madrid,
Barcelona, and Valencia—and squashed the rebellion's hope of
a quick takeover. Within ten weeks of the coup, though, Franco
was solidly in control of the uprising, with his major rivals either
imprisoned, assassinated, or killed in mysterious and fortuitous
airplane crashes.

The rebels designed their military campaign to be as violent,
brutal, and terror inducing as possible. The violence had a dual
agenda: 1) to encourage full capitulation to the takeover, and 2)
to "cleanse" the country of the Marxist scourge. General Emilio
Mola, the coup's original leader, avowed, "It is necessary to
spread terror. We have to create the impression of mastery [by]
eliminating without scruples or hesitation all those who do not
think as we do. . . . Anyone who helps or hides a Communist or
a supporter of the Popular Front will be shot" (Hochschild 2016:

31–32; Preston 2012; Thomas 2001). Given millions of Spaniards voted for the Popular Front, this was a terrifying threat and eventual reality for hundreds of thousands of Spanish civilians whose only crime was voting for the legal political party of their choosing (Hochschild 2016: 31–32).

The massacres occurred everywhere, even where the rebels met scant resistance to their takeover. Anything deemed progressive was suspect, such as being a Freemason or a vegetarian, learning Esperanto, teaching in a Montessori school, teaching peasants how to read, or being a member of a Rotary club. The violence was always ruthless and often indiscriminate. In Granada, rebels massacred five thousand, including one of the most famous missing Spaniards, famed playwright and poet Federico García Lorca (Graham 2005).

Almost all Republican mayors and politicians (who could not escape), union members and leaders, and an extraordinary number of local teachers, were rounded up, held in makeshift prisons, and then summarily executed. Many were killed in nighttime firing squads, while others were tortured before being shot, stabbed, or thrown from buildings or bridges. In the majority of cases, the victims of the extrajudicial killings were buried in unmarked mass graves, many buried facedown in unconsecrated ground.

The rebels had particular vengeance for women of the left, who were subjected to intense gendered and sexual violence during and after the war. General Gonzalo Queipo de Llano famously broadcast on the radio that the women of Madrid were to be viciously raped by Moorish troops and that "kicking their legs about and struggling [wouldn't] save them." Rebel troops wrote on walls, "Your women will give birth to Fascists." In Seville, soldiers raped and murdered a truck full of women prisoners, "threw their bodies down a well, and then paraded through a nearby town, their rifles draped with the murdered women's underwear" (Hochschild 2016: 38). It is assumed that the majority of female victims of the extrajudicial killings were raped before their deaths. (See, for other cases of rape as a tool of genocide, Goldenberg 1996; Snyder et al. 2006.)

In addition to the rapes, the rebels subjected Republican women, not just those killed, to gendered humiliation and torture. For example, the rebels, and later the Francoists, would shave the heads of Republican women, force-feed them castor oil, and then parade them through town—many times nude or partially nude—so locals could jeer at them as they defecated on themselves. The Franco regime continued this kind of gendered violence in the aftermath of the Civil War and the early postwar years.

The violence did not end after the rebels gained control of an area; rather, extreme repression, including imprisonment, torture, gendered violence, and humiliation, lasted well into the Franco regime. An estimated 120,000–140,000 civilians lost their lives in extrajudicial killings; their remains were buried in clandestine graves throughout Spain (Graham 2004; Renshaw 2011). In response to the escalating violence against civilians, around 440,000 Republicans or Republican sympathizers went into exile. At the end of the war, the Francoists aerially assaulted fleeing refuges as they tried to cross the Pyrenees into France. The refugees found little solace in France, and after the Nazi invasion were again in similar peril, with many sent to concentration and labor camps. After the war, Franco, in an agreement with the Nazi government, sent an estimated additional ten thousand Republican prisoners to Nazi concentration camps with six to seven thousand perishing at Mauthausen and Gusen before the end of the Second World War (Graham 2005; Preston 2012; Thomas 2001).

In the Republican-controlled parts of Spain, the news of mass rapes and killings led to retaliatory killings of those who supported the fascist takeover, mostly businessmen, landowners, and shopkeepers. The killings also included some clergy, who, for the most part, were thrilled at the idea of a Catholic regime taking over Spain. In total around seven thousand clergy members lost their lives during this period, with an estimated forty-nine thousand civilians killed in retaliation. Once they gained power, the Francoists used this leftist violence to insist that the war, the dictatorship, and the corresponding repression were all in the best interests of the country and a *legitimate* response to "red" terror.

From the beginning of the uprising, the Republicans were woefully undermanned, underarmed, and plagued with infighting from warring factions. The Republic, like the rebels, did receive some outside support, most notably from Soviet Russia, which provided outdated weaponry and some on-the-ground tactical support. They also received help from the famed International Brigades, volunteer military units made up of citizens of fifty-three nations. Their numbers have been estimated to be 32,000–35,000, with an additional ten thousand noncombatant volunteers (Thomas 2001). George Orwell, one of the most famous international fighters, wrote the book *Homage to Catalonia* about his experiences in the Spanish Civil War. However, that assistance was no match for the weaponry and financial aid provided to the rebel side by Adolf Hitler, Benito Mussolini, and the American Torkild Rieber, a Texaco executive, who provided key intelligence and much-needed petroleum (Hochschild 2016).

The Republicans tried to negotiate, but Franco demanded unconditional surrender. By 1939, the Francoists had taken the remaining Republican holdouts and controlled all of Spain. With the fall of Madrid at the end of March, the United States and Europe recognized General Franco as the dictator of the country and the war ended. In total, the war claimed five hundred thousand Spanish lives, with only one-fifth having died in battle; the rest were taken by air raids, disease, and execution (Jackson 2004; Phillips Jr and Phillips 2015; Thomas 2001).

Francoism

From the start, Franco moved to set himself apart and above all others in Spain. He did this first by becoming the "Generalis-simo" of the armed forces and head of state during an ornate ceremony. He then began to refer to himself, via his propaganda machine, as the "Caudillo" or "leader by the grace of God." Later he named himself Captain-General, a rank previously only held by Spanish monarchs (Hochschild 2016; Jackson 2004; Preston 2002). He also worked to rebuild the political institutions and policies of the country to reflect his vision.

Once fully in power, Franco declared there would be only one political party, the Falangist party, founded by José Antonio Primo de Rivera, who was executed by the Second Republic in 1936 for sedition. Franco's regime, and his Falangist party, wielded enormous and centralized power over the country in an attempt to create a "true" Spanish identity, which exempli-fied the qualities of discipline, personal sacrifice, religiosity, and patriotism (Jackson 2004). The regime brutally repressed any threat to this identity.

The regime, in its attempt to rid Spain of Marxism, aimed to create a unified, "pure" society that strictly observed the Catholic faith (Rodríguez Arias 2008). This included outlawing all non-Spanish dialects and exerting extreme repression in areas such as the Basque-speaking region in the North and the Catalan-speaking region in the East (Armengou, Belis, and Vinyes 2002; Jackson 2004; Phillips Jr and Phillips 2015; Thomas 2001).

Additionally, the regime believed that Marxism was an infectious disease to which children and women were especially susceptible (Armengou et al. 2002; Jackson 2004; Phillips Jr and Phillips 2015; Thomas 2001). Anything deemed Marxist or progressive was not only inferior but also a dangerous contagion to society as a whole. As such, the Franco regime focused on framing Republicanism as a contagious germ, whose spread was to be contained to protect the body politic of Spain, justifying the continued killing of Republican fighters and sympathizers alike. This logic also reinforced the idea of the biological transmission of Republican or progressive ideals from Republican parents to their children, making the institutionalization of Franco repression a multigenerational affair. (See Gal and Kligman 2000 for further discussion on the impact of nationalism.)

Franco's preoccupation with Spanish purity was due to the psychiatrist Antonio Vallejo Nájera, Spain's leading fascist thinker (Armengou et al. 2002). He was trained in Nazi Germany and was the Spanish army's chief psychiatrist, as well as a professor at the University of Madrid, and he later founded and was the director at the Bureau of Psychological Investigations, where he performed medical tests on prisoners in Spain's concentration camps with the intent of trying to understand how best to medically destroy Marxism. His theories were the basis of the Franco government's policy to remove the children of Marxist subversives from their parents, so as to prevent the pollution and deterioration of another generation (Navarro 2008). His theories were later used by the military regime in Argentina as the basis for their baby-stealing campaign (Rosenblatt 2015).

Franco initially implemented this policy of removal at the end of the Civil War when thousands of men, women—some of whom were pregnant—and children were interned in Spanish concentration camps (Armengou et al. 2002). The regime subjected pregnant Republican prisoners to torture, rape, and humiliation; some were executed after giving birth. At the end of the war, the women's prison in Madrid held almost fourteen thousand women, with many being raped and impregnated in prison. A series of laws passed in 1940 legalized the separation of children from their parents.

An estimated thirty thousand children, along with others who were incarcerated with their living parents, were affected by these laws and removed from the prisons to be placed in religious organizations or with families who supported the regime (Armengou et al. 2002; Rodríguez Arias 2008). The Falangist party argued that removing children from their parents' care was a noble and God-oriented cause (and in the best interests of the children and society). Many of the female children taken from the prisons were placed in religious organizations run by nuns, who viewed females as more corruptible, and therefore, in greater need of religious influence. Many of these young women renounced their parents and became nuns to pay for the sins of their families (Armengou et al. 2002).

However, the regime was not just suspicions of women of the left but rather believed *all* women needed to be strictly controlled. Like other fundamentalist regimes, the dictatorship was determined to undo any gains in gender equality. The regime banned coeducation, with one prominent party leader believing it to be a Jewish conspiracy. The state was intent on imbuing the "true" national character of its victory by mandating sex-segregated classes and manuals to teach boys to be "aggressive, violent, imperialist" and girls to be submissive homemakers who kept the "home ready for virile Falangist warriors" (Aguilar 2017; Hochschild 2016: 338; Lagunas 2017; de Mata 2009). Republicans and their descendants were either vilified or ignored in the official accounts, depending on the era, but were always characterized as an ongoing potential threat to the regime and to the nation. This common form of purposeful othering was used to maintain support of the repressive governmental rule and actions against enemy citizens (see De Grazia 1992; Irvine 1996).

Additionally, under the Franco regime, women were dependents on their fathers or husbands and needed their permission to own property, apply for a job, open a bank account, or travel at all. The regime, in its initial years, criminalized women who wore pants and banned them from attending university. Husbands had the right to murder their wives if they were found to be committing adultery (Hochschild 2016: 346; Lagunas 2017; de Mata 2009).

Shaming the Defeated, Franco Repression

During his initial years in power, Franco relentlessly punished and repressed the defeated Republicans. Immediately after the war, Franco declared the year 1939 to be enshrined as the "Year of Victory" in the official Spanish calendar. Additionally, he made all national holidays—excluding saints' feast days—victory festivals; he used them to rally loyalty for the regime and reestablish that the Republicans were inhuman communists deserving neither forgiveness nor compassion (Preston 2002; Renshaw 2011).

In 1939, he also passed the *Law of Political Responsibilities*, which justified the use of military tribunals, which the regime preferred; they offered the least amount of legal protection for the accused and often lasted only a few minutes. Through these trials an estimated four hundred thousand people were convicted of crimes against the state and sent to camps, prisons, or forced labor internments to do infrastructure construction throughout the country. The official numbers of those imprisoned do not include the more than ninety thousand people sent to "militarized penal colonies" where they were forced to work on a variety of local and state projects, such as building dams or canals used to irrigate the land on large estates whose owners had supported Franco (Hochschild 2016: 345; Preston 2002).

Franco famously signed sheaves of death sentences over lunch or coffee without reading the details. He would, however, ensure that the death sentence was vicious—often death by garrote—and that the executions received press coverage to ensure added humiliation, pain, and terror to the victims' families (Preston 2002: 42). His regime executed at least twenty thousand after the war, the victims' fates determined by military kangaroo courts, with possibly hundreds of thousands more dying in prison from neglect and disease. For example, in 1941, in Cordova, 502 inmates died in one day due to a lack of water (Hochschild 2016: 345). The killers buried the remains of their victims in local civil cemeteries in mass graves with no markers. Some victims, if they "confessed" to a priest, were buried in Catholic cemeteries.

Franco's repression was the most severe and widespread immediately following the war and into the late 1940s—perhaps in response to an ongoing militant insurgency of Republican fighters mostly living in the mountains. However, the use of illegal detention, enforced disappearances, and torture remained constant up until the end of the regime. The last few years of the dictatorship saw an accentuation of this kind of repression and violence due to increased militant actions by separatist groups such as ETA (Euskadi Ta Askatasuna, or Basque Homeland and Liberty). Part of Franco's ability to do this derived from the tactical and economic support he received from the United States government, who in the fight against global communism agreed to ignore Franco's previous relationships with Axis powers and continued human rights abuses in exchange for strategic military bases (Hochschild 2016; Preston 2002).

The regime banned all commemoration and mourning, including wearing mourning clothes, for those who died on the Republican side during the war and those executed and buried in mass graves during the immediate postwar era (Aguilar 2017; Renshaw 2011). Any kind of tribute, such as placing flowers on unmarked graves, was done secretly (Preston 2012). Scholars have argued that this total prohibition on mourning denied the victims' families the ability to practice very important cultural and religious death rituals, a particularly cruel form of psychic violence against the defeated population of Spain (Renshaw 2011: 66).

The regime also denied death certificates to many of the widows of the extrajudicially killed, making it impossible for them to remarry, adding an additional layer to their humiliation and suffering. Widows unable to remarry found themselves in an even worse financial situation within the extremely repressive and patriarchal society that limited the rights and work options of women (Graham 2004; Hochschild 2016: 345; Renshaw 2011). Many of these women scraped by through domestic labor, selling items and food along the roads, through secret charities, and the coercive actions of others (Renshaw 2011).

However, most of the repression the sympathizers and family members of dead Republican fighters suffered was the Franco regime's institutionalization of stigmatization and discrimination. The regime, to ensure that the Republicans suffered in all aspects, enacted a series of economic policies that effectively created second-class citizens. The institutionalization of surveillance, bolstered by legislation that essentially criminalized Republicans, included the creation of "certificates of political and religious reliability," which denied politically suspect persons and families access to work or travel (Davis 2005; Preston 2002: 44). Denunciations were common, and priests would take notes on who was or was not attending mass (Hochschild 2016: 345).

The regime seized the property and assets of Republican families, crushed unions, declared strikes as acts of state sabotage, and purged "leftist" professions (Davis 2005). War widows and orphans, or those wounded on the Francoist side, received pensions or jobs, while their Republican counterparts received nothing. These economic policies left the majority of Republican families unable to escape abject poverty. The regime also subjected the Republicans to an intense and vicious propaganda campaign, which portrayed the defeated as "bloodthirsty traitors against Spain" (Davis 2005: 862). The regime utilized the media, state events, rituals, and symbols, as well as the educational system, to maintain the demonization of the Republicans. The government also labeled Republican sympathizers as "Rojos" or "Reds," which became a common form of "othering"—often racialized in nature, which worked to label and repress both Republicans and their offspring for generations.

Creating the Dominant Narrative

Franco, like many other fascist leaders, strategically used propaganda, symbols, rituals, and festivals to ensure his version of the collective memory surrounding the war and the regime remained the prevailing narrative. Francoist propaganda was everywhere. The Falangist hymn "Face to the Sun" played every night on the radio and at all public events. All school-aged children were required to do military formations, raise the Spanish flag, pray, and sing the hymn before going to class. The process was then repeated at the end of the day (Preston 2002).

The Francoist state also had total control over news and entertainment media, ensuring that the Spanish people received a filtered perspective on ongoing political, economic, and social events in the country and abroad. Additionally, the regime ensured that school-aged children were only exposed to the regime's account of events by regulating the content in their schoolbooks, which ensured their account of the war was the only narrative; it even went as far as renaming the war "The Crusade" or "The War for Liberation."

Spanish public buildings in almost every town became locations of Francoist historical memory acts. The regime ensured that scrolls naming the Francoist war dead were ascribed to public buildings. Additionally, *all* Spanish churches put on their walls the name of the Falangist leader, José Antonio Primo de Rivera, a martyr of the Right. Moreover, some churches also affixed the names of local Francoist dead inscribed on crosses or displayed stained glass windows with the Falangist flag. Many of these commemorations remain on public buildings today. Since the return of democracy, the Spanish centralized state has never recognized the Republican victims in these ways.

The largest, most discussed Francoist monument to the dead is located at the Valle de Los Caidos (Valley of the Fallen), which is an enormous mausoleum where nearly thirty thousand Spaniards are buried. It contains a 262-meter-long basilica, a monastery, and a 150-meter-high cross that is as wide as a two-lane highway and took nearly twenty years to build (Preston 2002: 44). Approximately twenty thousand Republican prisoners—sentenced to reeducation via labor—built the Valley of the Fallen. Many of these prisoners were injured or killed during its construction. The style of the monument emphasized the regime's passion for restoring Spain's imperial strength and its desire to eliminate any lingering remnants of enlightenment thinking, even if only architectural (Preston 2002).

Primo de Rivera was the first to be buried at the Valley of the Fallen, reaffirming the space as one for those who fought and died valiantly in the face of "Red" terror. Originally, only those who had died on the Francoist side were interred at the site, but by 1959, it was open to those who had fought and fallen on the Republican side as long as they were Spanish (meaning no members of the International Brigades) and Catholic. The later requirement was usually impossible to prove due to poor record keeping or lack of interest by the Catholic Church. The regime exhumed both mass graves and formal burial sites from the Civil War, transferring close to seventy thousand remains to the monument. The regime then reinterred these remains alongside Primo de Rivera, and eventually, Francisco Franco himself.

Intriguingly, in the 1960s the regime conducted exhumations of Republican mass graves with the intent to rebury them at the monument. The regime conducted these exhumations without the permission, or even the knowledge, of the surviving family members. Some scholars have argued that this was done as a way to acknowledge the Republicans' efforts while controlling how they would be remembered (Rubin 2016). However, I posit that these exhumations are another example of how the Francoist state exerted its necropower; it wielded full control over the production and maintenance of its dead including how the dead were (or were not) incorporated into the larger identity and narrative of the purpose of the state's existence.

The interment of Republican remains alongside the founder of the Fascist Party, and up until 2019, is currently a point of contention in Spanish memory politics. Many organizations have demanded the exhumation and return of Republican remains interred at the monument, insisting that their loved ones should not have to spend eternity with their murderers (Rubin 2016).

Post Franco, Transition, and Changing Legal Regimes

In the 1960s, Franco began the process of opening up Spanish society to the rest of the world, which increased tourism and introduced more progressive social trends in popular culture (Renshaw 2011). In spite of some of these changes, the regime still maintained total control via repression and violence. The regime's last execution was in 1974. Thus, when Franco died in 1975 after almost forty years of rule, silence, censorship, and authoritarianism had become deeply engrained in Spanish political culture, making it nearly impossible to publicly raise issues regarding the violence of the past.

In 1973, the Basque separatist group ETA assassinated Luis Carrero Blanco, the right-wing hard-liner chosen to succeed Franco as the head of the military. As such, when Franco died in 1975 there was nobody who could succeed him. Consequently, Spain began a democratic transition in 1975 that ended in 1978 when the new constitution was completed. As the regime had constantly argued that the Civil War could be reignited at any moment, many Spaniards acted on this assumption during the transition to democracy (Aguilar 2002). Thus, Spanish political elites, "via the legal and institutional mechanisms of the old regime," orchestrated the democratic transition while attempting to ensure that another Civil War was impossible (Encarnación 2008: 60).

As part of that effort, the transitional government enacted the amnesty law of 1977; leaders in both the conservative and leftist parties brokered the law, asserting that the atrocities that had occurred during the Civil War and the Franco regime were to be forgiven and forgotten (Aguilar 2002). It was also referred to as the "pact of forgetting" (*pacto del olvido*), as it promoted censorship with the goal of building tolerance and preventing further political polarization in the country. This framing of the transition continued the marginalization of the victims of the Civil War and Franco regime and institutionalized a new form of sanitized silencing of the victims' suffering—purposely erasing and denigrating the histories of violence suffered by the victims by ignoring them until they were forgotten. This sanitization essentially allowed Franco's stratified system, with the victors maintaining structural and cultural power over the defeated, to continue. Some scholars have argued that the Spanish population internalized the pact of forgetting until the early 2000s (Aguilar and Fernández 2002; Encarnación 2008; Phillips Jr and Phillips 2015).

In December 1978, the transitional government ratified the current constitution, which defined the Spanish state as a parliamentary monarchy, with the King retaining the title of head of state. However, the majority of state power is divided between the central government (legislative, executive, and judicial branches), autonomous regions (e.g., the Basque Country, Cataluña, etc.), and municipal governments (specific cities) (Cabrero 2014). Democratic governance has been maintained since then, with the most serious challenge to it having been a failed military coup in 1981.

Changing International Human Rights and Spain

The pact of forgetting began its slow fade from symbolic and institutional power in the 1990s. During this period, academics, artists, journalists, entertainers, and everyday Spaniards began to somewhat broach the taboo topic of the past violence. However, in 1998, the judge Baltasar Garzón opened the door to major legal challenges to the amnesty and silence when he used universal jurisdiction to issue arrest warrants for Argentinean generals and for the ex-dictator of Chile, Augusto Pinochet. Pinochet had been receiving medical treatment in England when he was indicted for the disappearance of over three thousand people, including several Spanish citizens who were killed during the military coup d'état in 1973 and the military regime that followed (Encarnación 2007; Langer 2011; Sikkink 2011). Mass demonstrations demanding the extradition of General Pinochet were held throughout Spain, and the case was extensively covered by both Spanish and international news outlets (Davis 2005; Encarnación 2014: 140).[2]

Judge Garzón was able to use the international law of universal jurisdiction because the Spanish government had included it under Article 23.4 of the Fundamental Law on the Judiciary (*Ley Orgánica del Poder Judicial*) in 1985. This article granted Spanish courts the ability to take on cases related to the crimes of genocide, piracy, and terrorism (Wilson 1999). Another aspect of Article 23.4 was a residual clause that included jurisdiction over any crime that violated international treaties or conventions that Spain ratified. Spanish courts have interpreted this residual clause to include crimes related to torture, crimes against humanity, and severe violations of the Geneva Convention. In 1998, Garzón expanded the charges to incorporate human rights violations of Chilean and Argentinean citizens (Wilson 1999). This international incident sparked controversy both in Spain and abroad. Many found it hypocritical that Spain was condemning the acts of Pinochet and Argentina while continuing to ignore the crimes committed under Franco (Encarnación 2007). At this point, Spaniards actively began to challenge the heritage of silence and process the violence of the Franco regime (Aguilar 2008).

The Rise of the ARMH

One of those incensed by Spain's willingness to prosecute another country's war criminal without having addressed its own history of gross human rights violations was journalist Emilio Silva. In September 2000, he published an article entitled "My Grandfather, too, was a Desaparecido [Disappeared Person]." Silva, at the bottom of the article, listed his personal phone number. Later, he received a call from a physical anthropologist who wanted to help locate the remains of his grandfather (Renshaw 2011). In October 2000, Silva, along with a team of forensic investigators, located the mass grave containing his grandfather, Emilio Silva Faba, among twelve others, all victims of rebel forces in 1936. This marked the first time that an exhumation of Civil War–era dead were exhumed in a scientific manner and in accordance with international protocols for postconflict exhumations.

In December 2000, Silva, along with Santiago Macias, due to immense interest from fellow Republican dead descendants, founded the ARMH. Shortly thereafter, similar organizations and local chapters of the ARMH began to form around Spain. The ARMH, along with these other groups, became a loose network made up primarily of volunteers and citizen experts, who have been exhuming and commemorating Spain's missing. Scholars consider these groups (Forum for Memory, Aranzadi, local ARMH groups, Platform Against Impunity for the Crimes of Francoism), the main actors making up the Spanish historical memory movement.

Importantly, the ARMH has two wings to its organization. The first is the technical and scientific side, which attempts to stay as depoliticized as possible to protect the perceived "unbiased" nature of its technical interventions. This wing is much more prevalent during technical excavations and exhumations.

This sides also plays a small pedagogical role in homage ceremonies, with the lead archeologist often giving a quick review of the work done to find, exhume, and identify the remains.

The other wing of the ARMH is explicitly political and engages in making and negotiating political demands. The president and the vice president, as well as the people managing the social media accounts, mostly do this political work. As many homage and reburial events are public, the political wing often participates, either directly in the event or in a separate press conference. During these speeches, the political side of the ARMH will denounce the violence of the past, the silencing of the democratic transition, and the failures of the centralized state to address the past in a meaningful way. However, the ARMH does not associate with political parties and always reaffirms its advocacy as being on the side of the families of the victims.

The ARMH, among others, became so prolific in its work that in 2006 the socialist government declared that year to be the "Year of Historical Memory." In 2007, the government passed the historical memory law (*Ley de Memoria Histórical)* (Anon 2007). While important, the law was limited in many ways. Notably, it did not revoke the 1977 amnesty law and maintained that exhumations were private and individual efforts. However, the law did allocate limited state funds to be available for civil society organizations to conduct exhumations, thus paving the way for a large wave of exhumations that occurred between 2007 and 2011 (Ferrándiz 2013). As of this writing, across the various organizations conducting exhumations since 2000, over nine thousand bodies have been exhumed, with the ARMH and Aranzadi, the Basque forensic team, having conducted a majority of them (Torrús 2020).

In 2011, conservatives defeated the Socialist government. The new government promptly ended all funding for exhumations of

Civil War and Franco-era dead. The ARMH barely survived and has since relied on private donations, both domestic and international, and human rights awards. However, the ARMH, thanks in large part to the ongoing Argentinean universal jurisdiction case (further discussed in chapter 5), has received enormous amounts of press and donations, which have bolstered its efforts.

In the following chapters, I unpack how the ARMH uses a variety of tactics to challenge how Spain should remember the violence of the Spanish Civil War and the Franco regime. I demonstrate that these tactics weave together performative actions and pedagogy to introduce their reframed narrative of the past through the filter of depoliticized science, or perceived unbiased science as an arbiter of truth, as well as through moral claims about the rights of victims' families to recover and rebury their dead with dignity. I reveal that these actions also actualize new realizations and forms of posttransitional justice in a country where access to justice has been generationally denied. I begin with analyzing how ARMH workers use a variety of microinteractional tactics with local Spaniards during technical fieldwork to create the very social change that the movement is seeking.

2

EXCAVATIONS

A Scientific Trojan Horse

The September morning air is crisp and cool, the mist in the old cemetery slowly lifting in the fall sunlight. As an excavator tears into the earth, the tranquility of the morning evaporates. ARMH members and volunteers watch as the excavator creates the beginnings of a trench. The subsequent rows are about two feet apart and dug in a vertical manner. As the excavator removes layers of dirt, the team watches for changes in soil color, bone fragments, or other human artifacts. They are searching for two men executed by the Franco regime in the immediate postwar era. The son of one of the victims waits nearby.

The ARMH technicians in their jackets that blaze "ARMH" stand out against the hazy terrain. Nearby, along the wall of the old cemetery, lean their many tools—metal detectors, shovels, hoes, picks, and plastic boxes that hold smaller digging and archeological implements. While some of the technicians are watching the trenches being dug, others are putting up the association's official sign that explains their mission and the science behind their work. The poster is large, over six feet tall, and displays pictures of the victims as well as workers scientifically exhuming mass graves and analyzing human remains. In using

FIGURE 2.1 ARMH sign and information table for visitors at technical work sites

it, the ARMH hopes to spread the message of its work, promote talking about the past, and gather any new information from townspeople that could be useful in the search.

The old cemetery where they are excavating lies on the famous Camino de Santiago—a five-hundred-mile-long hiking trail that begins in France and was traditionally a Catholic pilgrimage trail. It also intersects one of the main paths into the closest town. Due to these roads, there is constant foot traffic from both pilgrims and townspeople. As the team waits for the dead to emerge, the town begins its morning routine. Like any new distraction in a small town, the sight of a large excavator ripping open the old civil cemetery draws a lot of attention. By mid-morning, a large group of older men and women from the village are standing around watching the work and telling stories about the violence.

This opening vignette illuminates the focus of this chapter, which describes how the ARMH's technical work acts as a foundation for breaking the silence and introducing a reframed narrative of the past. I demonstrate that in these interactions, even hostile ones, technicians are actualizing the social change they seek to create, breaking the repressive silence of the past, introducing reframed narratives of the violence, and destigmatizing the long-suffering victims.

When social movement actors engage with the social world in a performative way, they can demonstrate both their social situation and how they intend to change it; for example, African Americans in the civil rights movement actualized integration when they sat at white-only lunch counters (Bruce 2013; Butler and Athanasiou 2013; King 1996). Likewise, an ARMH excavation, as a performative action, converts the space into public places for the exchange of oral testimonies, or storytelling, about the past. Spaniards having nuanced public conversations about the past violence, the regime, the transition, and the current role of the Spanish state are all successful movement outcomes. Even if these conversations do not lead to the finding of a mass grave, the conversations actualize a micro-level interactional change and form of justice sought by the ARMH.

ARMH technical interventions additionally provide workers the chance to introduce two important movement frames: "the rights of the families" to bury their dead and the scientific approach that grounds their work in depoliticized science. This framing strategy helps get local buy-in, as it distances the technical work from the politics of the violence and takes the position that all families, as a basic human right, should be allowed to bury their dead. The depoliticized science frame fits within the rights of families to bury their dead because science is the medium for the retrieval and identification of the remains. The families' rights frame also hits upon key cultural values around death rites and proper burials that are particularly salient in rural Spain (Renshaw 2010, 2011).

BREAKING THE GROUND, BREAKING THE SILENCE

As one of the main goals of the ARMH is to recover the victims of the Spanish Civil War and the Franco regime, the group is rightly associated with exhumations. However, to be able to exhume a mass grave, one must first know where it is. The majority of the extrajudicial killings happened during the war, meaning that there is no record of the location of the graves or who is in them. Although the Francoists began keeping records in 1937, they did not always provide explicit enough details to locate mass graves; in contrast, for the executions that occurred during the first few years of the regime, the military often (though not always) kept detailed documents that included the names of the executed and their manner of death, autopsy reports, and their burial location. As such, ARMH historians spend months researching the circumstances surrounding disappearances or executions, including historical archival research, reviewing historical maps, and gathering any pertinent information from the victims' living relatives about their loved ones' premature death. When the association has a good sense of where the grave could be located, a team begins to excavate.

A team, however, still frequently faces many challenges while searching for graves in the field. For one, as the violence occurred over eighty years ago, the terrain has often changed topographically. For example, the construction of a highway or extensions added to cemeteries make locating graves difficult or even impossible. An example of this is the case of María Martín, whose mother was murdered by supporters of the coup in 1936 and buried in a mass grave with over twenty other people. Sometime in the 1970s or 1980s, after the transition to democracy, the government allegedly destroyed the grave when they built a new freeway over it. However, María, until her death, regularly placed flowers and held vigils for her mother on the side of the road (Junquera 2014). Her case highlights the long-lasting impact of state terror and that the physical location of a grave, even if it has been destroyed, is still a sacred place of remembrance for victims' families.

Technical Field Work

In cases where it seems plausible that a grave can be located, the ARMH will send out a small excavation team to search. All excavations begin in the same ritualized way and follow official

protocols; the lead archeologist maps out the confines of the
land that the association has official permission to excavate.[1]
This includes photographing and measuring the site. The team
digs trenches with shovels, though sometimes an excavator is
used. A backhoe will sift through the removed dirt searching for
any human remains, artifacts, or changes in soil color. If anyone
sees something in the trench, the archeologist will examine the
area more closely.

The team's technical work follows the script of traditional
archeology and international mass grave exhumation protocols.
The reliance on protocols reinforces the ARMH's scientific team's
position that they are archeologists and technicians first and fore-
most, which protects the validity of their later findings and their
positionality. In addition to protocols, the team, during both the
excavations and exhumations, wear a variety of clothing appropriate for the changing natural elements and outdoor labor. They
also have an assortment of tools. Their clothing often displays
"ARMH" or the ARMH logo on the back, front, or the pockets.

The majority of these excavations occur near the sides of
roads or highways; team members are legally required to wear
reflective bright green neon vests, rendering them quite visible.
In many ways, their use of tools and clothing, though functional,
also serve as props and costumes that help break the silence of
the past.

ARMH excavations often occur in small villages, especially
in the northwest of Spain where the association's laboratory is
located. The ARMH actively seeks the presence of locals at the
technical work sites because the goal is to encounter more witnesses who can help locate a grave or fill in additional details
about the violence. The group is hopeful that more victims'
families may be interested in searching for missing relatives and
will come to make the initial contact during the technical work.

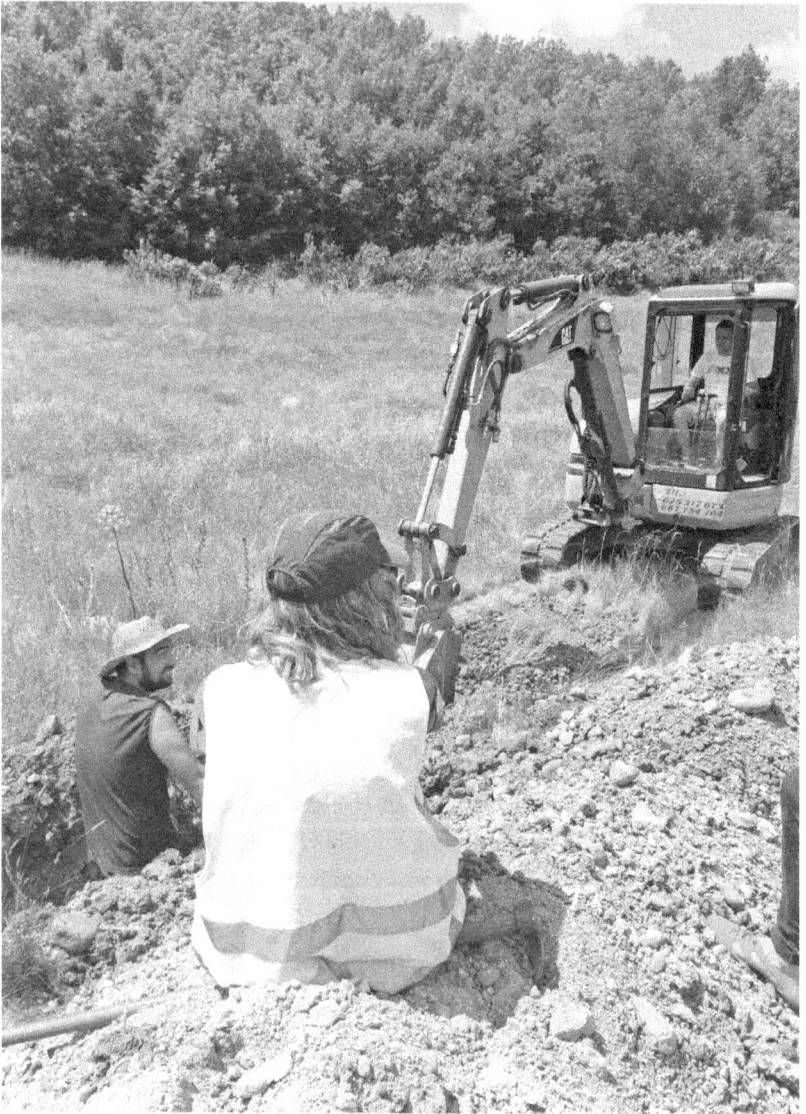

FIGURE 2.2 ARMH technical team excavation

To make this happen, the ARMH contacts newspapers in advance about its work with special attention dedicated to the victims who are in the grave and the location of the search, so people will know where to go. Most visitors will have heard about the ARMH's work through the newspaper, which, especially in smaller towns, is the key media used to communicate the association's work and purpose across all age groups, as opposed to social media or word of mouth.

Furthermore, locals often know the histories of violence in these small towns even if they are not spoken about publicly (Renshaw 2011). Locals' knowledge about mass graves and their locations makes the graves only truly clandestine "in the official negation of their existence and the silence imposed on communities" (Sanford 2003: 17). The appearance of workers digging near, or at the location, of a known grave empowers the ARMH to retake public space in the excavation of memory and the breaking of this silence. Thus, locals, seeing work near a known grave, will often approach the team to talk or ask what they are doing. The interactions that happen at and around the excavations— the performance of science—begin important social processes of actualizing the societal changes that the ARMH hopes to create—namely the breaking of the repressive silence of the past and the destigmatization of the victims.

When locals approach the team, the ARMH's historian or a volunteer will greet and try to engage them, especially if the individual is older. After confirming that the team is indeed searching for a grave, villagers tend to have a wide variety of reactions. Some, like an elderly man named Alvaro, respond with a deep and pained sigh saying, "What a shame this was. I just don't want another war." His reaction is illustrative of the fear that is still salient in many of these small villages, the fear that memory movement actors, like the ARMH, are trying to combat.

Yet, in spite of these fear-based concerns, villagers walking by almost always ask about the science of the work. The technicians and volunteers, happy to chat, explain the basics of the international protocols they are following, what tools they are using, or why the lead archeologist is staring so intently into the large holes made by the excavator. In one such exchange, a group of older women, on their way to the market, remarks, "It's just like on TV with those detective shows!" Again, the ARMH's reliance on protocols, including their clothing and tools, reinforces their positionality as scientists doing their job. It also helps to liken their work to that of state crime technicians working a crime scene, not unlike detective shows on TV. These shows (like *Bones* or any of the *CSI* spinoffs), though problematic in many ways, help make forensic science accessible to nonprofessionals and carry the suggestion that a crime has been committed. What is important is that locals perceive the ARMH as being on the same technical level as the science detectives on television. Whether this is accurate or not is, in some ways, irrelevant.

Moreover, following protocols and professionally doing their work suggest a level of comfort with what the ARMH workers are doing. They are not going about their work in a rushed or anxious way, or as if the work is a radical act against the state. As one of the ARMH leaders explains, "People are silent because of fear. One way to resist the continued impunity and fascism in this country is to show [the people] that we are not afraid, and they should not be either. It is incredible what a simple example of that can do." This model of behavior, as explained above, helps to normalize the space and is a conscious choice. Again, it was not just the regime, but also the democratic transition that maintained the repressive, sanitized, and still salient silence of the past, which preserved the hierarchy of victors, the vanquished, and pervasive fear. Performing their work calmly makes the space approachable. Additionally, piquing the locals' interest creates a twofold outcome: 1) the ARMH can get more information to help find the graves, and 2) it creates aspects of the social change and justice that the association wishes to see.

Public Spaces and Testimony

Public spaces have long been credited as important for the facilitation of political discourse, critiquing the state, and helping to maintain participatory democracies (Habermas and de Launay 1978; Azevedo 2016). Technical fieldwork, especially an excavation, creates this kind of public gathering space for townspeople to witness the work of the ARMH. The copious amount of free time technical work provides, in addition to volunteers' willingness to listen, also helps to facilitate the engagement in cathartic storytelling. As the Spanish government has yet to engage in any kind of truth and reconciliation interventions, long considered a universal aspect of peacebuilding with almost every "emerging state from authoritarian rule or civil war," there is a lingering need for this kind of action (Nauenberg 2015: 654; Phelps 2014). I suggest that the temporary public places created by ARMH technical fieldwork, at least partially, fill this void. Obviously, the impact of these small gatherings is not the same as those organized by the state. However, in small villages, I argue that there is an unpresented value to these interactions, even if it just means people are allowed to speak publicly.

Intrinsically, townspeople who stay to watch the technical work will often organically, with very little prompting, start to recall what they know about the violence. These stories frequently focus on cursory and terrifying tales of violence against women, violence perpetrated by the church, generalities about the suffering, and criticizing the state's past and present memory politics.

At one excavation, in the Castilla y León province, a rainstorm caused all but the four paid team members to huddle under a canopy. While the storm raged, the locals, as well as some relatives of the victims, recounted stories their grandparents and parents had told them. Their accounts were about the people in the nearby village, including the locals' own relatives, who were murdered or had fought in the war on the Republican side and eventually succumbed to the Francoist forces. For some in the group, it was the first time they had told these stories outside the safety of their homes.

Sitting under the tarp, one of the local men started to tell a story with these words: "But you know the women always suffer the most." A woman in his village had been forced to watch her husband's murder during the uprising in 1936. He continued, implying through a series of well-timed pauses, that she had also been a victim of sexual violence. Later, during the regime, her property was seized by the local Falangist party, jeopardizing her economic survival. The woman, to survive, then had to prostitute herself to the same men who had killed her husband.

At another exhumation in the northwest region, locals, including victims' relatives, came to visit the technical fieldwork. One man in his mid-seventies came every day to speak with whoever would listen. One day, a group gathered around him as he explained how the rebels had executed his relatives, along with others in the town, throwing their bodies into a well. The perpetrators were his neighbors. He went on to explain how the Francoists then imprisoned his teenaged mother and his grandmother. All the women of his family had their heads shaven, were force-fed castor oil, and were then paraded around the town as they vomited. His story also hinted at sexual violence. The storytellers almost always insinuated sexual violence without ever expanding on it. Rather, locals used a sort of shorthand, such as saying things like "you know what happens to women." It was also expected not to press them for details, as it would be too painful for them.

Others focused on the violence of the Catholic Church. During an exhumation that I analyze in chapter 5, many stories were told of an assassin priest who wore a black glove on his left hand. After prisoners were shot to death, this priest would deliver a second bullet into their heads to ensure they were actually dead, a practice he was said to enjoy.

At another excavation, a man arrived in the company of the local priest. He announced very loudly to all the people standing around him that this priest was okay: "Not like the other one." The priest of the village during the regime was vicious and had used his power to take both property and lives from the "Reds" in the village. Discussing the Catholic Church's involvement in the violence, especially in front of a priest, would have been very difficult before the historical memory movement's inception in 2000. Yet, even in this instance, some listeners looked a little nervous until the priest nodded and said, "That man was shameless and not a true man of God."

At other points, the public space of the excavation provided a way to start destigmatizing the victims and creating space for others to express solidarity with the families' rights to recover and rebury their dead, as well as process the fear imposed by the state. At one excavation that turned into an exhumation, the locals came every day to see the work; they hung around the metal barriers that separated the technical work from the public, with some older people bringing small stools to sit and watch. It was in this space that the locals began to recount their own memories, or the stories they heard from their parents or grandparents, about the war, the violence, and the transition, facilitating a platform for public storytelling. The older villagers sighed and ruminated over the pain and suffering caused by the war, many saying they believed the families had the right to rebury their loved ones. In one conversation, an elderly man in his eighties, Pablo, gestured to the victim's family, who were watching the excavation, and remarked, "They have suffered enough."

Others, like Juan and Rosa, a married couple in their sixties who had read about the ARMH's work in the newspaper and had driven an hour to see it, spoke about the repressive silence of the past. Juan said, "It was just total silence." Hearing that, Carlos, another local man in his sixties, interjected, "It was a terrified silence. To speak would be to risk everything." He continued talking with Juan: "The democratic transition was just a continuation of the regime." Rosa and Carlos both nodded in agreement. Carlos added, "So it did. It maintained the silence." Like many others, they agreed it was simply incredible to see the ARMH's work. Later, as the conversation wound down, Rosa said, "I hope they find them, so the family can finally have peace and rebury their father." The rest of the group solemnly nodded in agreement. The right of a family to rebury its dead is a powerful frame, as it sidesteps why there is a body to recover in the first place. Importantly, it refocuses ARMH's aim, and that of the larger forensics-based human rights movement, toward the simple goal of family reunification, even in death. That frame clearly resonated with the local community and helped to maintain support for the ARMH in the town.

ASKING FOR HELP: TACIT MECHANISMS THAT FURTHER PROVOKE BREAKING THE SILENCE

Another aspect of technical work–related interactions is compelled collaborative community work, which occurs when the ARMH needs help finding a grave. As previously mentioned, locating graves can be difficult even with extensive research. When this happens, the ARMH will attempt to get locals to participate in the search. Though the team often already has a contact person in town to rely on for information, sometimes it is necessary to ask locals what they know about the past. In this section, I unpack these more intrusive interactions.

Compelled Community Collaboration

Throughout my time in the field, every excavation or exhumation I have observed has included some form of testimony gathering from people living near the gravesite. Unlike the previously discussed interactions during technical fieldwork, these exchanges are more assertive, often involving just walking up to people in small towns and asking them if they know where the mass grave is located. As one might expect, this technique can be hit or miss. However, that does not mean these conversations do not accomplish something important. In fact, these interactions force locals to break the silence and reckon with the violence of the past, all under the guise of needing more information. The ARMH leadership often strategically asks foreign volunteers or researchers to do this work since they are seen as less threatening. As one leader said, "People aren't afraid of talking to [foreigners]" because they are not perceived to have a side.

In one instance, all the international volunteers were driven to the local village—population of around seventy—and dropped off in the town square with notebooks. The town had a long history of right-wing politics starting with supporting the rebel cause and later the Franco regime. The first woman I spoke to brought me to the church, which was right off the main plaza. She pointed to the portraits of three priests hanging on the wall and said, "All killed by the reds." We continued to speak about the past and the point of the exhumation. She eventually said she thought she had heard that the grave was off to the side of the road and might be hard to find.

After this conversation, I ran into the local postal worker, and he was more than happy to engage. He was in the middle of doing his rounds, but he suggested I go see the pharmacist—who apparently was also a hobbyist historian—as well as an elder of the town whose family had been terribly repressed. As we were chatting, an elderly man in a motorized wheelchair came up to us. Upon asking him what he knew about the grave, he said, "The past should be left in the past"; he did not believe in exhumations as "they were opening up old wounds." He then went on to tell me all the stories of the violence that rocked the town in 1936 and through the war. Interestingly, his testimony, like almost all I had gathered in that town, had a reoccurring theme: after the killings, people had seen dogs running through the streets with arms and legs in their mouths. Locals described this detail repeatedly, as an example of total terror, even for those who families were not killed. After recounting the story of the dogs, he then told me where the team should be looking—up in the mountains, where the road bent.

Locals' confession of knowledge as to where the grave was located, even if it took a little time to admit, seemed to stem from the desire to help, or at least be part of what was happening in the village. Regardless of motivation, the very fact that locals were conversing with strangers or other villagers who might not share their political viewpoints was the actualization of the breaking of the silence, as well as an acknowledgment of the existence of victims. These conversations also forced locals to recognize their town's very violent history, express the terror of those stories, and possibly confront the complicity of their ancestors.

Others were quite open to the ARMH's presence in the town. One group, three women and one man who were all in their early fifties, had read about the association's work in the newspaper. Paula said she had been told the stories as a child, which included how "all the 'reds' were rounded up in the town square then thrown into the back of a truck. They drove up that the mountain over there, shot, and thrown off the bend." She continued, "You know? They say that for weeks after the dogs were running around with arms and legs in their mouths. Can you imagine? Arms and legs!" She then suggested the team look for the grave at the bend on the mountain road.

We then discussed what the group thought about exhumations. They all agreed that they were a good thing and that the families had the right to find their missing relatives, as a form of needed closure. Not one thought of the ARMH's technical work as political because, as Claudia said, "They are just trying to help people bury their relatives. There is nothing wrong with that." Rodrigo agreed, saying, "It's important for families. I don't think it's a problem." The fear that exhumations would open up old wounds, bring back the violence, and lead to the downfall of democracy did not bother this group of friends. Rather, the idea that families have the right to bury their loved ones was a more compelling reason to support scientific exhumation efforts.

However, fear was still very salient for the victims in the town. As suggested by a few of the locals we spoke to, we headed to the house of the village "Red" to see if he had any information, but he refused to speak to us other than yelling, "Leave the past in the past! Just leave them alone already." Later the ARMH sent its original contact person, who was a neighbor of his and a leftist. At this point, the man gave his testimony to the Spanish members of the team. In this circumstance, the elderly man, even though he wanted to help, was terrified of strangers asking questions about the past, especially since they had been seen speaking to others in the town.

Later I reencountered the postal worker, who asked how it went with the village elder. When I explained, he responded, "For some the war is not over. It is still happening for them." These examples highlight both the progress and the continuing struggle for the historical memory movement. The majority of the town did break the silence of the past and offered up personal stories of what they knew under the guise of helping the team find the grave, even when they did not agree with exhumation work. Yet, in the case of the elder, the town Red, he was, at first, too scared to talk. However, after he saw that he was safe, he did decide to speak, and did so on his front porch, in full view and defiance of his neighbors.

In other instances of compelled collaboration, perpetrators of the violence also asked to participate in helping to find a grave.[2] An example of this occurred when the team was searching for a mass grave of at least twenty-five people that was thought to be located in a large field alongside a highway. Locals called the area the "Valley of the Dead." When the team was more than a week into searching with no success, they sent the historian and a foreign volunteer into the surrounding towns. They found an older man in his late nineties who lived nearby. He had been a soldier in the Francoist army and had helped bury some of the dead. After hearing about what the team was doing, he said that he wanted to help the elderly son of one of the victims find the remains of his father. The victim's son was only a few years younger than he was.

When the ex-soldier arrived, he walked around the site and used his cane to point out to the historian the location of various other graves that he knew existed, many located across the road from the excavation site. He said that where the association was looking was a waste of time. Almost two weeks later, the team discovered he was right. The ARMH never found the large grave they were looking for but did discover two smaller graves on the other side of the road containing the bodies of five men and one teen-aged boy who died alongside his father. As it did not have official permission to excavate all the locations the ex-soldier had pointed out, it is likely that more graves line that particular highway.

Though the ARMH considered it a success to find the two graves, the failure to find the designated victim's grave, in many ways, compounded the grief for the aging son and his family. Not only had the ARMH failed to find the grave, the family now also faced the reality and agony that they had been leaving flowers in an empty field for almost eighty years. The man said it was like losing his father all over again.

Compelled community interactions force locals to openly think and talk about the country's violent past and also the more personal violence that occurred in their town. These interactions also encouraged locals to see the actual excavation site in person. ARMH workers, by getting the locals to participate in helping in the search or by telling stories, also led them into becoming part of the new history of Spain.

Hostility and Destigmatization

As expected with difficult historical themes, the ARMH's excavations did not always elicit good feelings in the villages.

Sometimes locals responded with immediate hostility. At an excavation that lasted over ten days, a few of the team members went to a local café, and sitting at a table nearby were three people in their thirties and forties. They were discussing the excavation not knowing that a group of ARMH technicians (myself included) were right next to them (no one was wearing ARMH-affiliated clothing). One of the two women of the group said, in reference to the victims, "I do not understand why they are putting so much effort to find *those* people. They should be made into the foundations of buildings and left there." The man in the group agreed. "They are just going to open old wounds. Why can't they just leave things alone?"

Though I was unable to start a conversation with this group, the idea that excavations and exhumations of the Republican dead would not only open old wounds but could cause the return of violence is a common antihistorical memory talking point. In my formal interviews with nonactivist Spaniards, most had faith that Spanish democracy could withstand discussing the past. However, many still openly worried that politicization of the memory movement and the pain from the war could bring back, if not violence, rancor and societal tensions, which could be dangerous. In one interview with Esme, a woman in her sixties, and her daughter Laura, a lawyer in her thirties, both articulated support for the memory movement, but had serious concerns about "opening old wounds." As Esme explained, "Yes, I think people trust the democracy and now if you talk about these things, you can go have a coffee with someone you are fighting with about the past. However, it just seems to me if we open these things back up and do not let the people forget for some time that we are going to return to another war, which is why I think we should write history two hundred years after wars happen."

Her daughter, Laura, however had a different view, saying, "I have the perception that with one jumping spark all this could all return at any moment. But for the people, above all, my generation, we lived closer to the war in Bosnia . . . and I believe that societal fractures are much closer to us than we want to believe. . . . But I worry that these kinds of movements heat up society on both sides."

Esme agreed, saying that it wasn't necessarily talking about Spanish Civil War that was potentially destabilizing to the nation, but war in general. She continued, referring to watching Bosnian war videos, "That's the thing, you see these things and [pause], listen, life is the way it is, and it is never going to change. There are always wars and the way things are now in [the] world, well . . . I just hope we never live this." However, in spite of these concerns both Laura and Esme agreed that families should be able to recover their loved ones as a form of reconciliation, as it may help to get "get rid of the pain" and potentially the future seeds of war.

Others used the "leave the past in the past" argument as a shield against potential stigmatization. Isabella, a thirty-something local server in a popular restaurant and bar, started our conversation by stating she was completely against excavations happening nearby, saying, "I don't know why they are opening up old wounds." Even though Isabella was born after the transition, she had clearly internalized the official old state line, at least initially. However, her story was more complicated than blind belief of sanitized silencing or in maintaining the hierarchy of victors and losers. As she continued speaking, she offhandedly said, "Well, my grandfather is in a ditch somewhere; he was a republican mayor in the village over." When asked if she would ever want to recover his remains, she became anxious and started to slowly rip up a napkin saying, "Oh, no. I do not think that the family would like that, though it would be nice to get him out of the ditch. But who knows where it is?"

As we continued speaking, she began to soften her stance on the ARMH and the recovery of remains, like those of her grandfather. By the end of the conversation, she said, "Well, now that I know more, I think it is right that the families have the right to recover their loved ones." She also liked that the exhumations were scientific and not tainted with politics; rather, they "were about helping families move forward." Yet, she maintained that her grandfather would likely stay buried because her family would either find exhuming him distasteful or potentially shameful to admit to their Republican history.

Isabella, like many of the locals I spoke to in northwest Spain, appeared to carry the burden of shame, or at the very least wariness, of being associated with Civil War politics or Republican family members, at least initially. However, the ARMH's focus on the rights of the families and a scientific approach provided the chance for locals to endorse the ARMH's work without risking being labeled "Red" sympathizers or agitators looking to disrupt the social order.

An additional value of the interactions provoked by the ARMH's performative technical work is its ability to destigmatize, or at least begin the process of destigmatizing, the victims. Throughout this chapter, I have illustrated how the interactions between villagers and ARMH technicians conducting fieldwork create opportunities to discuss the past violence, whether by asking for help or locals organically telling stories about the violence while watching the work of the team. In addition to the actualization of breaking the silence, these interactions also rehumanize and destigmatize the victims. The stigmatized identity of being a "Red" in many instances can become, in Erving Goffman's terms, a "discreditable identity," as it can be concealed or hidden (Goffman 2009). Nevertheless, in the case of village life where one has always been associated with the stigmatized group, being a "Red" is a "discredited identity," or an identity that cannot be hidden. As such, working to reverse this stigma can come from confronting those who want to maintain these societal inequalities.

A useful example of this came from a story from Blanca, an ARMH volunteer who participated in the Guadalajara exhumations in 2016 and 2017. One day during the first few weeks of the first exhumation in 2016, she recalled seeing Maria Jose, a woman in her late seventies, approaching the grave. She was wearing a fur coat, big earrings, and looked "well put together." Following behind her were two female relatives of the victims, their heads down as though they were scared and ashamed. As the three got closer, one of the relatives, Martina, tried to warn Blanca by making faces.

The well-dressed woman then directly approached Blanca and coldly demanded to know what they were doing. Blanca explained that the workers were attempting to remove the bodies of "assassinated Franco repression victims." Maria Jose then spit out, "I think this is ghastly. What you are doing is indecent. You have to know that [people on] the other side were just as murderous." She went on to say, "In fact, I have a brother who was murdered by the reds. They buried him somewhere and no one knows where." Blanca responded that if the woman wanted to give her all the information she had on her brother's death that the ARMH would very much like to help her find him, explaining that the association does not only search for victims from one side of the war: "If he is in a mass grave, we will look for him." Maria Jose declined and continued saying, "No, the only thing that you are doing here is removing shit, literal shit." Blanca responded, "No, they were not shit. They were victims, they were human beings who were murdered, and maybe you don't agree, but what we are talking about here is human rights and the rights of the families." The woman got very angry with Blanca and eventually stormed off, yelling to all those listening, "You are removing shit!" However, in our interview, Blanca, explained why she thought this interaction had been important:

> During the entire time, Martina was behind this woman, she had her head down. She was listening to me talk about the valor of the victims and that they had been assassinated, murdered—by the time the other woman left, Martina's head was up, completely up. It gave me the sensation that this was the first time that Martina could lift her head up in front of this woman—listen they knew each other. [Maria Jose] was a wealthy woman from the same village [as Martina] and had relatives implicated in the violence. So, of course, Martina always had her head down in front of her! She *had* to keep her head down in front of people that spoke like that, in front of the winners. So, when Martina saw for the first time, someone dignifying her relatives and someone standing up to these people, while also standing firm about what *actually* happened in the past, it felt like I was watching someone who has lived their entire life with their head down and then had the chance to [raise] their head up. To have the strength to look directly at the people who never had to live their lives in fear for what happened. She did that. She watched that woman leave. And, I believe, no, I know that she never dropped her head for this woman again or for anyone who thinks like her.

In fact, at the second exhumation about a year and half later, Martina continued to visit the team. She would regularly bring homemade pastries and coffee to keep everyone warm. She no longer exhibited fear and willingly spoke to the local and international press about her family's experiences as well as her own. As Blanca argued, it seemed that Martina lost her fear through watching someone stand up to the bullies of Francoism.

In this instance, and by far not the only one, a person who wanted to maintain the established order did not intimidate the ARMH worker into silence. Instead, she held her ground and provided an example to the repression victims standing nearby. The interaction between Maria Jose and the ARMH worker, Blanca, threw off the normal hierarchy of Martina's stigmatized identity, putting Maria Jose into the unaccustomed position of retreat. As for Martina, considering her later actions and behavior in 2017, having someone humanize and defend the victims as being worthy of care and respect helped her to develop her own identity as an activist, unafraid and happily speaking to the press.

Conclusion

This chapter has demonstrated how ARMH excavations, like the one in the opening vignette, become temporary public places for performative microinteractions where locals can tell these stories of the past. These exchanges, including those compelled by ARMH workers, actualize the social change that the larger historical memory movement is trying to create in Spain, notably breaking the silence of the past. This chapter has also illustrated how these interactions create an opportunity for destigmatizing the long-suffering victims.

Moreover, conversations, storytelling, and supporting the "rights of the families" to recover and rebury their loved ones is a form of justice that is accessible to the victims' families, especially in the context of continued amnesty and disinterest from the centralized Spanish state. Spaniards, by talking about what happened during the war and regime in their immediate villages, bring a personalized awareness of the past, as opposed to an abstract understanding of what happened. Likewise, these conversations break the official negation of the victims, which maintains a hierarchy of winners and losers that prioritizes silence. Furthermore, storytelling shares the responsibility for restoring justice in postauthoritarian and postconflict societies (Herman 2015: 210). Scholars have similarly argued that "people need to have the truth of their and their family members' lives acknowledged by both their neighbors and by those in power," which requires the "telling, listening, acknowledgment, and concrete manifestations of the acknowledgment" (Phelps 2014: 842). Hence, individual stories, even seemingly small or insignificant historically, can—especially when combined with the scientific evidence found and presented in mass grave exhumations— expose a "larger history of structural violence and political opportunism" (Phelps 2014: 843). Restoring justice to postconflict or postauthoritarian societies can only begin if people can share their stories and talk about the past.

State terror is not just about terrifying its direct victims but also all those who witness it. As we know from other scholarship, this terror is then passed down intergenerationally (Hirsch 2008; Kellermann 2001). This chapter has demonstrated how microinteractions between ARMH workers and locals actualize the demystification of this terror. This implies that whether you have a crowd at an excavation site telling stories or a technician walks up to people watching and asks them to help find a mass grave, these interactions end the silence and the official negation of the dead's existence, as well as break the power of terrified silence. These interactions provide a public opportunity to release the terror of these disturbing stories. Speaking about the violent past acknowledges that it happened, that it is over, and that there is space to keep processing it.

In the next chapter, I discuss how the ARMH invites locals to come to the site and listen to impromptu classes led by ARMH leaders when exhuming a mass grave. Unlike during excavations where the technicians encourage local visitors to tell their personal stories about the past, during these classes, ARMH leaders use pedagogy to teach visitors the "true" history of Spain via forensic science. Additionally, these classes allow for the embodied remains and the victims' personal objects to "speak" their truth, humanizing the victims and reframing the stories of their deaths.

3

AT THE FOOT OF THE GRAVE

Teaching Science and the "True" History of Spain

As discussed in the previous chapter, fear and silence about the past are still a lived reality in many parts of Spain, particularly in small towns. Like other technical work, ARMH workers must be careful during exhumations with their approach to the topic of the past violence. The technicians also want to protect their image of being legitimate sources of information and not political agitators bent on destabilizing the democracy.

In this chapter, I discuss the structure of ARMH's impromptu classes given at its mass grave exhumations.[1] Technicians begin by framing their work as pedagogically oriented since they are teaching the forensic science that helps explain the more complex history of Spain. I demonstrate how technicians deploy the "depoliticized science" frame, which grounds their work in science rather than politics. By using a depoliticized approach in their human rights activism, ARMH technicians are able to sidestep delegitimization strategies used to discredit their agenda due to the perceived "unbiased" nature of forensic science. Moreover, ARMH technicians frame their work as being about educating fellow Spaniards about the "true" history of Spain, making it a matter of education and pedagogy, not politics.

FIGURE 3.1 ARMH archeologist leading a class at an exhumation

Additionally, this chapter reveals how once their work is grounded in depoliticized science, technicians then weave in claims about the rights of the victims' families to retrieve their loved ones' remains. Moreover, I illuminate how the ARMH class leader allows the activated objects, such as bones and personal objects found in the graves, to "speak" their truth. I illustrate how at this moment the objects transform into the embodied lives of the dead, which allows ARMH technicians to make sharper critiques of the Spanish state's memory politics and introduce claims for the need for transitional justice. In the final section, I show how the impact of the classes can lead to participatory democratization of collective memory.

CLASSES AT THE FOOT OF THE GRAVE

Visitors often do not have to go far to look, as ARMH exhuma-tions normally take place off main roadways or in civil parts of local cemeteries, wherever the mass graves are located.[2] Depend-ing on when the locals arrive, the team can be either in the pro-cess of uncovering the bones or removing them. However, in order to protect the grave and the workers from the elements, workers put up tarps, canopies, and physical markers near the grave, such as red-and-white tape, which help both to delineate the grave's margins and also create a boundary line to which visitors can approach.

The team will be aware that visitors may be nervous to approach, not only because of Spain's history of repression, fear, and silence, but also because human remains are fully visible during exhumations. As such, the workers try their best to create an open and welcoming atmosphere at the burial site by greet-ing every visitor and engaging with them on a personal level. Visitors very rarely come alone and are often accompanied by friends or family members. The ARMH can have more than ninety people visiting a grave at any given time. The team's engagement facilitates connection and reduces the sometimes overwhelming emotions that can appear when one is viewing a mass grave for the first time. A team member explained, "One of the most important goals of creating an open environment is that everyone, even those who are against our work, feel wel-come to approach and interact."

Visitors often approach slowly; many stay a good distance away from the grave until encouraged to approach. I have observed a variety of emotional reactions in visitors approaching a grave for the first time, ranging from stoic silence and gasps to hands over mouths. Intense curiosity often inspires the visitor to lean in closer for a better look. As one older man said, "*Que horror, que horror* [what a horror, what a horror]. . . . I can see exactly how they were thrown in. Time stopped when they buried them." This description is accurate—when viewing a mass grave, at least concerning well-preserved skeletonized remains, it is quite easy to see how the killers buried the bodies. If the bodies were not previously disturbed, they are in the exact positions where they fell and are sometimes still wearing the clothing or accessories they had on when they were killed, such as wedding rings, shoes, belts, hair combs, etc. It should be noted that remains with clothing, other than traces of cloth, are very rare, as textiles tend to degrade faster than metal or rubber.

Once a critical mass of visitors has arrived at the grave, ARMH leaders begin an impromptu class, which, in spite of its spontaneity, usually begins with a crash course in forensics. Often the lead archeologist starts by explaining that the team is following international protocols created by the United Nations on how to exhume mass grave victims and that the ARMH grounds its work within the international human rights norms and discourse. The leader will then explain that through forensic anthropology, combined with extensive historical research, it is possible to know certain facts, such as whose bodies are in the grave, their sex, and age ranges, as well as whether perimortem (occurring at or near time of death) injuries exist. The forensic archeologist or other trained class leader then explains how forensic anthropology is used to differentiate female and male skeletons by looking for various osteological differences, like the width of the pelvis or the back notch of a cranium. If there are both female and male skeletons in the grave, these differences can easily be demonstrated. Politics, the leader will explain, never affects their findings, as the protocols, and the science itself, do not allow room for an identified objective or political bias to enter.

The leader then weaves in the known history of the victims and how they died, using the research of the ARMH's in-house historian and oral testimonies from relatives and locals. In some cases, some of the more gruesome details, such as testimonies of intense torture, including castration or rape, are edited out, so as not to overwhelm the visitors. However, sometimes those listening, especially if they are locals, will lean toward whoever is close and fill in the missing details.

The class leader then segues into explaining an exhumation's various technical stages, beginning with the stage of the excavation (the removal of dirt on and around the remains) or the exhumation (the removal of the bones from the gravesite) that the team is in. For example, he or she sometimes draws attention to specific team members and explains the various tools they are using, the parts of the body they are working on, which areas of the corpse are more difficult to excavate, and the importance of the painstaking nature of the work, all before describing how the bones will be cataloged and wrapped in newspaper, put in boxes, and transported to the laboratory for further analysis. A volunteer forensic anthropologist will later analyze the remains following international protocols, after which the team will hopefully be able to identify the victim. The leader explains that reclaiming a body's biological identity is an internationally recognized human right and is one of the most important aspects of the ARMH's work.

Sometimes identifications can be procured from forensic anthropology and archival work alone, such as one case where the victims were a mother and son. Once the sex of the bodies was determined, the remains were identified. Other times, victims can only be identified through DNA testing. For many years, the ARMH had to pay for DNA tests because there was no national DNA database, state support, nor Spanish genetic laboratory that had offered to do the work pro bono. Due to this, the ARMH could not perform genetic testing until, as the course leader says, "the Argentine Forensic Anthropology Team (EAAF), one of the most important and influential teams in the world" took over the ARMH's DNA testing needs for free because "they believe in the work of the ARMH."

The leader's focus on explaining the technical nature of the work and the ARMH's international connections and support solidifies and legitimizes the association's claim that it is an internationally recognized science-based organization and not outwardly motivated by politics. This focus reinforces ARMH workers' authenticity as educators who inform the people about the team's work in "recovering Spain's true history based in the evidence found in the grave." By doing this, the ARMH is alerting those listening to the fact that a renowned international human rights organization, the EAAF, believes in and trusts the ARMH with the goals of bringing international human rights norms and science to Spain.

This emphasis on the science and pedagogy of the work also functions as a more focused introduction to depoliticized science, which grounds the validity of the work in internationally recognized scientific methods. The science and the protocols being introduced by the leader are presented as being agendaless and depoliticized; they are simply the arbiters of unearthed truth. Once this credibility and legitimacy have been established, ARMH technicians can more easily navigate the rewriting of the collective memory of the past, which they do by then describing to the class how families can contact the association to find and exhume their missing loved one.

INTRODUCING MORAL CLAIMS

To gain access to the ARMH's expertise, the victim's family must first make a formal request, giving official permission to the association to search for and exhume, if possible, the body of their relative. Then the historical archival work, which includes requesting official documents, such as birth and death records, if they exist, from the local government, begins. This process can be long, as some regional governments are opposed to this work and engage in stalling, but due to the historical memory law are eventually compelled to comply. When it is determined where the person died, the association will search to locate the grave or speak with locals about the grave's location. In many cases, luck in finding a grave depends on when the killing occurred. It is easier to locate it if the killing occurred during the Franco regime, as they documented their actions.

The leader will remind everyone that the association's main goal is helping families of the victims of state terror recover their relatives and bury them according to the families' cultural and religious beliefs. They tell every class, "The most important part of our work is the reinternment. We do this work so that the families and *not* the killers get to decide how the victims are buried." The leader continues by stating that the association does not believe the families should pay for any of the associated costs of the search and recovery of their relatives, but rather the state should be responsible; however, "as the state is not paying, we [ARMH] have taken over their responsibility." They explain that the ARMH does not make any of the reburial decisions; this right belongs to the families, "a right that has been denied to them for eighty years. A right all families deserve." However, the ARMH does offer to hold a commemoration event before the reburial if the family wishes (detailed in chapter 4). The ARMH always defers to the family's wishes on the details of both the commemoration and reburial to ensure that the family is supported in every way possible. The ARMH even provides headstones for later cemetery burials.

The leader's focus on the moral imperative of the rights of families has long been the ARMH's stance and something for which it has received criticism (see Bevernage and Colaert 2014). However, the tactic of focusing on the families, their suffering, and the very human need to honor the dead rather than the politics that led to their relative's deaths is a useful tactic, as it neutralizes opposition to the work. By doing so, the ARMH is tapping into long-existing cultural norms surrounding death rituals and the obligations of families to their dead kin (Ferrándiz 2013; Hertz 2017; Renshaw 2011). Moreover, it is a working strategy, as seen in chapter 2.

Any critique of the state is also tempered, as ARMH is suggesting that the state should be responsible for helping victims move forward, not demanding that the state be overthrown, pay reparations, or even apologize. However, this is not to say that the classes are completely depoliticized. As pointed out by team members in interviews, the politics are always there, making it unnecessary to make explicit references to it. As one principal of the association said, "Everyone who comes to see the graves knows that this was political violence. Everyone knows at least that. Why is it necessary to hammer the point and potentially run off curious people who are afraid of being associated with 'red' politics?" This quote suggests that the ARMH leadership is strategically depoliticizing their work in the hopes of reaching more people and therefore having a larger societal impact, and in doing so, the ARMH is quietly helping to change the discourse of collective memory.

Additionally, this part of the class frames the work as being apolitical, as the team is working at the request of victims' families, conservative or liberal. Thus, the ARMH frames itself as a venue for the will and agency of victims' families, not a political organization with explicit political goals. An ARMH leader's emphasis on the victims' families also places scientific exhumations as *the* medium for families and communities to gain much-needed closure for wounds that never healed, as opposed to a political act motivated by revenge or the desire to destabilize the country. That framing also connects the association's work to the larger international forensics-based human rights claims that all families have the right to recover their missing loved ones as a form of justice, and that the victims of enforced disappearance have the right to be repatriated with their identities.

THE GRAVE SPEAKS

The classes, especially if the audience sees skeletons bearing marks of violence, are already providing authentic counter-memories because the skeletons do most of the talking. The literature on objects and their impact on individuals and groups, or materiality, is deep and rich. Materiality studies see the material world not solely as an incarnation of ideals and values but rather what gives social relationships meaning, structure, form, and limitations (Griswold, Mangione, and McDonnell 2013; Zubrzycki 2017). This perspective also allows objects to have agency as expansions of personhood that create reactions from social actors (Gell 1998; Zubrzycki 2017). As such, materiality studies attempt to understand the dualism between objects and subjects to illustrate how social relations are developed through material culture (Griswold et al. 2013; Zubrzycki 2017).

Building on this perspective, but coming from science and technology studies, actor network theory (ANT) provides a powerful venue to analyze materiality and how objects can have "a voice of their own" (Latour 1987). According to this view, objects are not simply acted on but can influence action directly as this power is distributed among actors, human and nonhuman alike (Akrich and Latour 1992; Griswold, Mangione, and McDonnell 2013). These nonhuman actors, also known as *actants*, affect behavior via how humans and nonhumans interact with each other. For example, nonhuman actants, whether it is border control policy (De León 2015) or an art museum layout (Griswold et al. 2013), can change how humans (such as migrants or museum visitors) respond to them, thus creating new ways of interpreting and classifying the world (Griswold et al. 2013). This theory helps trace how people and objects work together in the stabilizing of scientific findings as well as give power to particular ideas.

In this case, the ARMH, through its pedagogical explaining of the technical work at mass grave exhumations, sets into motion a specific kind of interaction between the visitors and the nonhuman actors found in the grave, specifically human remains and embodied personal objects. Thus, these classes, including the historical and forensic facts taught to the visitors, work *with* the objects in the grave to give the past a "voice" that stabilizes and empowers the ARMH's counter-narrative of the past. The technicians also act as necessary translators for the objects, using forensic and historical information to help give meaning to the objects' agency. As such, when the story of the physical remains of a person who was shot execution style and buried in a ditch alongside the highway is being told by a trained forensic expert, the skeletons "speak" the loudest. No further political commentary is needed; the remains are already clearly articulating it. Furthermore, starting the second part of the class with the presentation of evidence of violence signals the beginning of a clearer criticism of the Spanish state and seizure of its sovereignty over the collective memory of the past while simultaneously actualizing justice through the truth of exhumations.

THE BONES "SPEAK" THEIR TRUTH

After discussing the technical work, the class leader shifts the class's attention to any objects found in the grave, usually starting with bullets, bullet casings, or the clear presence of bullet wounds in the remains. As the visitors pass around bullets and casings, the leader declares that these objects "are clear signs that a crime has taken place, but"—pausing for effect— "it is impossible for any of the families to receive justice due to the amnesty law of 1977." The Spanish state, as a further insult, has ensured that the educational system and government continue to ignore the past. Drawing from personal experience, the leader tells the group that not once during his education, including while earning his degrees in forensic archeology and history, did he learn about the Civil War, the dictatorship, or the fact that "Spain is second only to Cambodia in terms of how many mass graves exist in the country."

Spanish law requires that the Civil Guard, or the state police, be contacted anytime there is evidence of a crime having taken place. Thus, the ARMH always submits a report to the Civil Guard after an exhumation, which often results in the Civil Guard visiting the graves to further document what's been found. However, due to the amnesty laws they are unable to investigate. This form of political theater sometimes causes tension, as the Civil Guard during the war and dictatorship were responsible for many of the killings and disappearances. Not surprisingly, the guards can be quite unsympathetic, if not downright hostile, to the association. However, by filing the reports, the ARMH forces state actors to visit the graves, observe the violence, and then publicly declare their inability to investigate due to the amnesty laws, which reinforces the importance of the ARMH's role, its narrative, and the willful impotency of the state to address the past violence.

The leader then directs the focus to signs of violence on the bodies, such as bullet holes or perimortem fractures, and explains how it is scientifically possible to discern the difference between entry and exit wounds (see figure 3.2), although sometimes visible holes can be caused by other sources. Through my observations, I noticed that visitors are drawn to clear signs of violence, such as a bullet wound to the skull or a chest cavity filled with bullets. Visitors often attempt to get physically close to the skeletal remains to see the wounds and ask for explanations about what they are looking at, for which they receive a technical answer. Bodies with clear signs of violence have less ambiguity, which allows visitors to more clearly hear the voice of the remains, their materiality. The technical answers additionally strengthen the ARMH's positioning as the true translators of the remains' voice and Spain's violent history.

In my informal interviews with visitors, many would say that bones with signs of violence spoke the "true" history of Spain. At one exhumation, a local woman in her late sixties came to see the grave with her sister after reading about the exhumation in the local newspaper. She explained, "I had to see it for myself. After all the stories I heard growing up . . . I just had to see for myself what was done to these boys. I had to know." The woman continued, saying that what she saw— the bullet wounds in their skulls—was more violent than she had expected. She maintained that in spite of this she was glad she came because she wanted the dead to know that they were being met

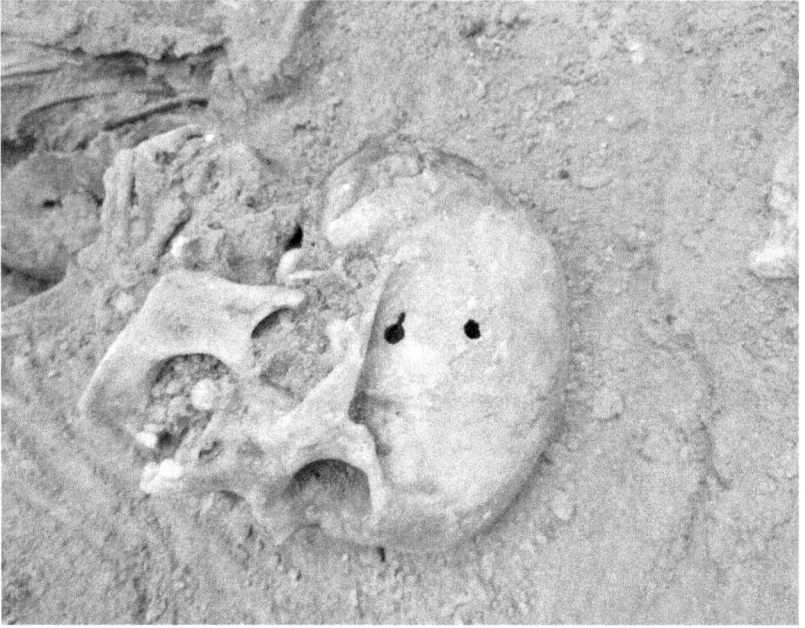

FIGURE 3.2 Remains with clear signs of violence

with kindness and that hopefully they could be returned to their families. She thought all Spaniards should be required to see the graves and that the bones spoke more loudly and honestly than any politician. In this case, the clear, materialized voice and agency of the remains worked to solidify this woman's understanding of the past, which echoed and gave immense power to the ARMH's framing of the violence.

Many of the visitors I spoke with also cited skeletons showing signs of violence as being some of the more moving aspects of visiting the exhumation and tended to write about it in the visitor's book. In one book, a woman wrote, "I was so impressed to see the skeleton and the cranium with the little bullet hole. What feelings of emotion were running through my body, and the tears forming in my eyes! I hope that the families can finally receive the news that their loved ones have been found." Another man wrote, "It is unbelievably impressive to see the bullet wound in the head. Your work is a moment of light for those who were impoverished by the darkness of a bullet." Yet again, these writings suggest that the materialized voice and agency of the remains containing bullet holes are clear and eloquent. The story the remains are telling is that these deaths were violent actions of state terror. Moreover, these findings suggest that those who are listening to the "voices" of the remains are interpreting them in the way that the ARMH has framed them. As such, the ARMH, using science, is providing clear truths via the use of scientific protocols to reveal evidence, such as bullet wounds. Additionally, the bones themselves are speaking their objective truths in strong voices. Together, these methods culminate in the amplification and reification of the ARMH's reframed narrative of the past, an actualization of the movement's goals and eventual justice.

EMBODIED OBJECTS, EMBODIED LOSS

For many visitors, family members, and team members, personal objects also become "embodied" with the imagined lives of the dead. Embodiment is the idea that a feeling or concept—or in this case, the dead—can become visible and tangible. Scholars have shown that human remains have the capacity to trigger emotional responses, as objects of mourning, from both relatives and witnesses alike (Renshaw 2011: 460).

While some people viewing mass graves do not emotionally connect or feel affected by the human remains (Cassia 2005), personal objects or clothing can create a feeling of intense connection, as the personhood of the deceased becomes powerfully represented through the physical objects (Crossland 2013). Personal belongings, accordingly, can conjure emotional and embodied moments, which facilitate relationships among the living and dead. These connections transform the objects into a tangible reality, allowing them to be easily imagined as having been used in life (Renshaw 2010: 457). Wagner (2008) similarly argues that personal objects found in graves in Bosnia and Herzegovina recall a life, a person, and a story.

I contend that the objects and remains found in ARMH-led exhumations are so powerful because they embody the lives of the dead and emphasize and amplify the "story" the technicians and remains themselves are already telling. The classes then use these embodied objects to encourage those in attendance to humanize the vacant skeletons, so they can be seen as humans, as victims, who died in a moment of state terror. Additionally, the classes help to reinforce that these people are worthy of being remembered and cared for, as opposed to forgotten, which, according to the ARMH, has been the state's perspective for eighty years.

BREAKING THE SILENCE AND ADVOCATING FOR ACCOUNTABILITY

After discussing signs of violence, the class leader then calls attention to a personal object in the grave. Throughout the course of my fieldwork, almost every grave exhumed contained personal objects belonging to the victims. The most common objects to survive eighty years in the ground are metal objects (such as rings, clasps, buckles, etc.) or shoes, likely made out of leather and with rubber soles, both of which take longer to degrade.

During one exhumation of four people (two couples), the leader pointed out a wedding ring, hair comb, and red earring still resting on the cranium of a twenty-three-year-old female victim (see figure 3.3); according to locals' testimonies, she was eight months pregnant at the time of her death. After pointing out her personal objects, he asked the group, "What kind of threat was this woman to the state that could have justified her execution? How can it be that the government also says that this woman and her relatives would be unable to receive any kind of legal justice for her murder? Or that her story, among the more than 120,000 stories of the disappeared, should never be told?" At a different class, he displayed the remains of a black leather shoe that had degraded enough to reveal the foot bones of a teenage boy who died alongside his father (see figure 3.3). Again, he asked the class, how were the violence, the silence, and the impunity justifiable?

In my interviews, respondents frequently mentioned personal objects as being one of the most impressive and moving parts of the class. One woman, who attended the class with the boy's shoe, began crying when the leader pointed it out. Later on, she explained, while holding on to her ten-year-old son she brought with her to the exhumation, she was overcome when she saw

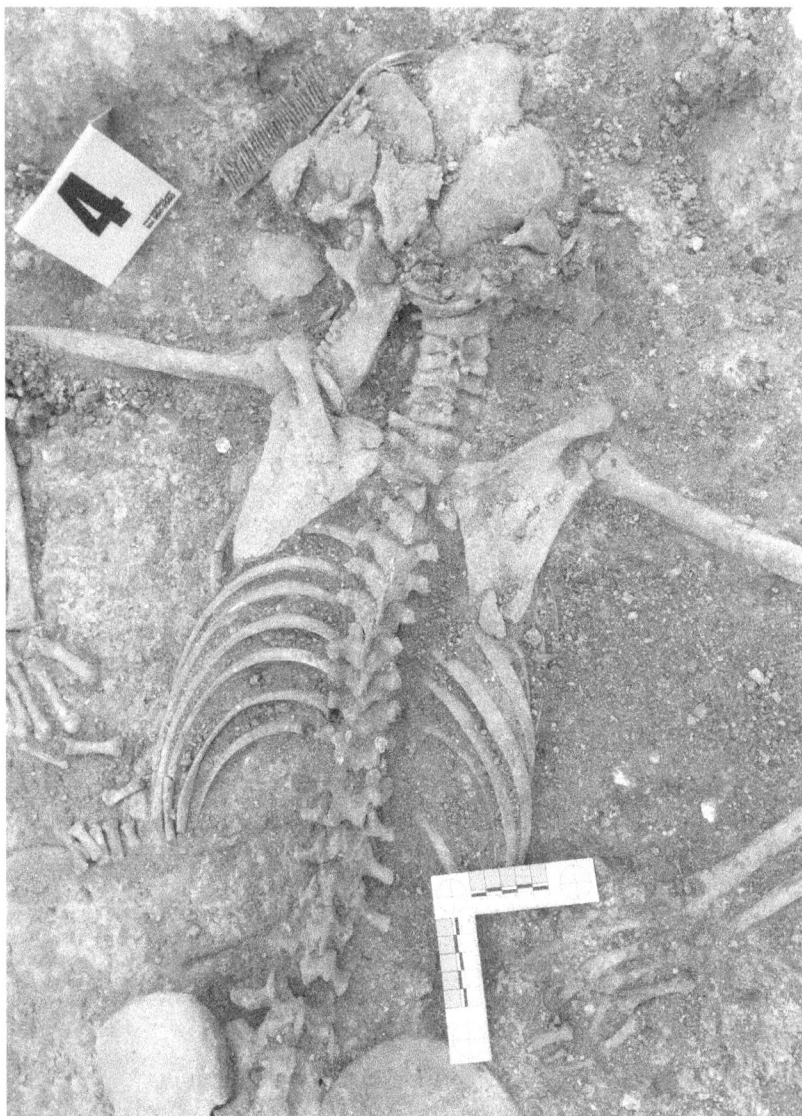

FIGURE 3.3 Personal objects found in graves—red earring, hair comb, and shoe

FIGURE 3.3 (*Continued*)

the shoe because "those were the shoes that boy died in." Here the embodied life and death of a child via his shoes helped to facilitate an emotional connection with a visitor. Moreover, this moment of embodiment—the unjustifiable murder of a child at the hands of the state—also facilitated a connection to the remains and their agency. The visitor described the boy in the grave as "a child not that much older than my son."

Team members also noted personal objects as being one of the more difficult and provocative elements of their work. During one interview, a female worker explained how at her first exhumation she was surprised that she felt nothing. She explained that it was not until she saw a pair of shoes with the heels worn down in a similar way to how her boots wear down that she began to feel the impact of the work. She said, "It wasn't until that moment that I understood them [the remains] to be humans who had lives. This person had been walking—in the same way that I walk—they were having a life and then it was over, taken from them for no reason." She then became so overwhelmed with grief that she had to leave the gravesite until she composed herself and could return to work. Another team member was so emotionally affected by the pregnant victim with the red earring that he later incorporated the image of the earring into a tattoo, thereby turning his body into a permanent homage and locus for further "teaching moments."

This level of connection to individual victims through personal objects was not limited to visitors or team members but also affected the victims' relatives. As with excavations, families of the victims are often deeply involved in searching for their loved ones, including staying graveside during exhumations. At one exhumation in a small village in Galicia, a part of Spain known for concentrated repression, the association was exhuming two bodies. One of the bodies was discovered still wearing detailed blue-and-green art deco cufflinks. The victim had been a local tailor who had been interrogated by the Civil Guard about his knowledge of the rebels living in the surrounding hills. His final moments of life were brutally violent, as his skeleton revealed many torture-induced premortem fractures.

During an interview following the exhumation, one of his grandsons explained that while he had not known his grandfather or his family's full history up until now, he was grateful to have been able to, along with his cousin, "meet his grandfather" and learn his family's history through the story of his bones. It was important to him, as a sign of respect, that they remove his grandfather's body from his clandestine grave. He maintained that the cufflinks were beyond meaningful saying, "What a beautiful remembrance to have. What a beautiful way to connect to him . . . I cannot wait to take them home with me. That way we will always have him with us." For the grandson, the cufflinks embodied the life of his grandfather and were a way to feel a deep emotional connection to him.

Personal objects are able to humanize the victims because they facilitate a material connection to the past; they tell the story of the life that was lost in a very clear and simple way. If a skeleton is still wearing a pair of shoes with soles made out of tires, it is easy to see the life of a poor yet clever peasant who made shoes that would last. A wedding ring speaks to the existence of a spouse, possibly children, and a home life left behind. A pair of earrings or a hair comb tells the story of a woman and her preferred fashion style. These objects sketch out the basic outlines of a life, of a person.

This embodiment of the objects is intensified when they are presented in combination with the basic historical and forensic facts about the victims, such as their age and sex, or the discovery of fetal remains or torture-induced fractures. Furthermore, these embodied moments merge with the voiced materiality and agency of the remains so that the message is loud and clear. This combination allows the personal objects to embody not only the imagined lives of the dead and what was lost with them but also the horror and cruelty of state terror. Additionally, as these moments of embodiment are being realized, the witnesses are also looking at a hole in the ground containing the skeletonized remains of murder victims whose violent deaths are easily imagined, thus making their last moments of life even more real and terrifying.

As such, the ARMH technicians draw on the power, agency, and translated voice of the recovered remains and objects. This voice of the embodied action-oriented objects then stabilizes and strengthens the ARMH's counter-narrative of history. As the visitors look at the objects, they transform into the embodied dead, thereby intensifying the visitors' emotional connection to them and the narrative explaining their existence. This approach is an extremely effective one-two punch that leaves visitors with a visceral and affective experience of the past violence.

THE PUBLIC'S EMOTIONAL AND POLITICAL RESPONSES TO THE FORENSIC LESSONS

At the end of every class, the leader asks if anyone has any questions, starting a question and answer session. The majority of the time the visitors have a standard range of questions: What will happen next? How do you DNA test the bones? What happens if you cannot identify them? These questions are answered relatively rapidly with a quick rundown of the following technical steps, including a review of the anthropological and genetic tests to come, how they are done, and what happens when someone is or isn't identified. If a victim is identified, ARMH plans the reburial based on the family's wishes; if identification is not possible, the remains will stay in the laboratory until they can be identified. However, visitors often use the question and answer sessions to process emotions or express political opinions. In many cases, the first emotion expressed by visitors is gratitude.

After one class at the exhumation of four victims who had been killed in 1949 during a shoot-out with the Civil Guard, some locals used the question and answer session to express both gratitude and contrition for the past. Unlike many of the other exhumations I attended, these victims of state violence had not been disappeared, nor were they citizens of the village where they were buried. Rather they had been living in the mountains ten years after the Civil War as guerrilla fighters battling the regime. The regime fully documented their deaths, conducted autopsies, and then buried them in individual caskets in the civil part of the cemetery. According to local legend, each victim had been buried in a red casket, as they were "Reds." Additionally, many of the elders who attended the exhumation were the children of those who had been responsible for the violence that led to the four deaths.

At the end of the class, an elder from the village who had attended every day of the exhumation, raised her hand to speak. She turned to the victims' relatives, including the daughter of one of the victims, and said, "I want to thank the team for their tremendous work. I want to thank them for allowing us to close this painful chapter in our town. It is very emotional to see this. And to the families, I want to say I am sorry for what was done to yours. They were not bad like they said, and neither are we. We are sorry for what happened here and hope that you will now have peace." When she went over and hugged each of them, others from the town followed her lead and approached the families to offer similar sentiments and hugs. One of the relatives responded to the outpouring of support by announcing, through his tears, his gratitude to both the team and the town for allowing them the opportunity to retrieve the remains of their loved ones and for "helping us close this wound in our family."

In this case, the class worked to facilitate the reframing of the state-created narrative of violence, which was that this violence was necessary to take down a violent communist guerrilla threat. As well as reframing the narrative into one of unjustified and brutal state terror, the class gave a public venue to the children—on both sides of the violence—to facilitate a mixture of connection, atonement, and the beginnings of closure.

Many of the villagers of this town were very affected by the violence that had occurred. During my informal interviews, locals expressed how the exhumation gave them an opportunity to express both their sadness and feelings of guilt over the past, as well as relief that this chapter had finally ended. For some townspeople, this opportunity was extremely important, as they wanted to apologize, ask forgiveness, and show the relatives their humanity; they wanted to be seen as distinct from their parents. The families of the victims were overwhelmed by this show of support and felt grateful that they had been able to participate, with one female family member happily taking pictures with the villagers and team members for her family photo albums.

In other circumstances, visitors used the Q and A sessions to make explicit political statements and connections, which the ARMH's technical team does not officially engage in during its work. During one exhumation in the south of Spain, where the class included more than ninety people, all but one of the responses were politically oriented. The first man to speak started by saying he wanted to recognize the work the team had done, as a relative of a victim. He continued by saying that this village had always been filled with humble working people, as proven by what was found in the grave (one of the victims was wearing shoes made out of old tires). He pointed out that this village had no attacks against churches, as did some other towns, nor had the local Second Republic officials extrajudicially killed or imprisoned anyone. He said that the fascists who had carried out the violence in this town had done so out of undeserving revenge. He wanted to recognize the work of the team and asked everyone listening to applaud the work that had been done to recover the remains of the victims. The entire crowd applauded, including the team members. In this case, the local, after viewing the bodies and listening to the class, was reasserting the ARMH narrative that these were unjustified killings and that the exhumation had revealed humble and innocent victims of the state.

During the same session, a well-known Civil War historian asked to speak. He was also a repression victim. His physical body testified to the brutality of the regime; he was on crutches due to a childhood battle with polio, because children of "Reds" were denied access to vaccines. He began by thanking the team for their work in finding four more of the lost. He then launched into the history of how many were killed in this region of Spain, how many graves are still unopened, the importance of remembering what happened in the past, and remembering them as victims of fascist state terror. He went on to say, "Each Spaniard needs to see these [exhumations] to be *informed*. We need to be informed about what we are looking at [pointing to the grave;] there are four cadavers, the remains of four people who were assassinated. . . . The people of Spain need to see this clearly, so that they understand what happened. . . . It is not valuable to hear or see our history *decaffeinated*." He ended his speech by repeating the common refrain of many global memory movements: *"Nunca mas!"* or "Never again." The leader, after the historian was done, introduced him to the group as a prominent scholar who had helped create a list of the missing in Andalusia, and who had been helping the association locate many victims.

In this case, the question and answer session became an extension of the class, as the historian led it, which helped to reinforce the ARMH's pedagogical and scientific legitimacy and the counter-narrative of the violence. Additionally, as the ARMH technical workers are positioned as scientists, and are being received as such, they are also distanced from the politics of the dead and the visitors. Rather, the ARMH is perceived as helping, as the historian said, to inform Spain of its real history, and not in a "decaffeinated way." It is then up to the visitors, or the witnesses, to decide what they think is the real history of Spain. Moreover, the visitors are the ones making the political statements, not the ARMH. The ARMH is thus somewhat distanced from the consequences of these opinions.

Democratization of Collective Historical Memory

Not all question and answer sessions were supportive of breaking away from the status quo. At one exhumation, a retired judge attended. After the class, the judge began by first thanking the team for its work. He then asked a question about the efficacy of justice and whether the Spanish state was actually obligated to do anything under international law. The judge maintained that the amnesty law was just because it had maintained peace during the democratic transition, and to hold judges accountable for failing to help victims' families was unfair. At this point, some of the other twenty people in the class began to murmur disapprovingly. It should be noted that something as simple as disapproving public murmurs would have been impossible only a few years ago, as this was a powerful man during the regime.

As the judge continued to argue against the need to change any of the judicial structures, even contesting the need for judges to have any part in exhumation efforts, a woman standing near him interrupted. She asked him, while gesturing to the remains, how he could say these institutional silences were just? The class quickly became a group discussion over the role of the judiciary, and what needs to change—or does not—to achieve justice. Another visitor stated, "The remains clearly show that a crime has taken place, look at the bullet holes!" One ARMH volunteer, a woman in her early thirties, jumped into the conversation to say that if it were not for a judge, she would never have been able to exhume her grandfather. In fact, she continued, her grandfather's case was the first in Spain to be supported by a judge and "without the judge's support he would still be buried in a ditch like a dog."

The judge eventually capitulated that families should have the right to retrieve their dead and that respecting that right is important for healthy democracies. This discussion continued and covered the role of the Spanish state, the politics of the democratic transition, as well as how the victims should be remembered, including a brief dialogue over defining the victims as civilians or "rebels" who died in battle—with some scoffing at the idea that they were rebels. The conversation ended with everyone agreeing that this was the time for Spain to finally acknowledge its violent past. What was particularly poignant was that this negotiation of collective memory occurred directly in front of the exposed remains of six victims of state terror.

I asked about this exchange later in a discussion with team members. One suggested that this conversation was emblematic of all of Spanish society. He said, "Here you have the institution, the judge, who is interested in maintaining the status quo and is not interested in investigating or pursuing justice. Then you have the local people who are listening to the judge, most scared to say anything, with the exception of [a] small, but vocal, group of people, most of whom have been directly impacted by the violence. Then you have the left and the academics (the ARMH), and they just stayed silent." However, while this may be an accurate interpretation of the failings of the various actors in the historical memory movement, the fact that some of the locals felt that they could disagree and engage in a *public* debate with a person of institutional power is a sign of progress. Additionally, by not participating in the debate, ARMH leaders maintained their explicit depoliticized stance while conducting technical work.

They present and frame this aspect of their labor as being the pedagogical medium of Spain's true history, not its political leaders.

This debate, as well as the group contrition shown in the first vignette of the chapter, reflect the impact of these classes. In both cases, locals felt empowered enough to push back and have meaningful conversations, using the information recently learned to back up their positions. Although some stayed silent, they were also watching, and they were provided with a valuable model of how to have these kinds of discussions, as well as what breaking the silence without fear looks like. Additionally, those silently watching also did not witness any serious or dangerous repercussions for breaking the silence. Since a fear of breaking the long and institutionalized silence, whether grounded in logic or not, is pervasive in rural Spain, this demonstration is powerful. All these examples contribute to restructuring how history and collective memory can be better understood and expressed by citizens and the process can shift from a top-down approach to one that is more participatory and democratic.

Conclusion

This chapter has demonstrated how the pedagogical structure of ARMH's impromptu classes held at its mass grave exhumations produces the opportunity to introduce "depoliticized science" framing. By using that approach, ARMH workers can both sidestep delegitimization while simultaneously weaving in moral and judicial claims about the rights of the victims' families to retrieve their loved ones' remains. I have also illuminated how ARMH class leaders let the activated objects, such as bones and personal objects found in the graves, "speak" their truth, which allows the objects to transform into the embodied lives of the dead. From here, ARMH workers can introduce sharper critiques of the Spanish state's memory politics, make claims for the need for transitional justice, and open up the space to the participatory democratization of collective memory.

The findings of this chapter further elucidate how exhumations, and the role of forensic experts, create new forms of justice, such as teaching the truth found in the graves to local communities. Without the forensic explanations and signs of violence that appear on the bones, the skeletons would be speaking a foreign language to the majority of the visitors. By positioning themselves as the scientific experts, ARMH technicians become the official voice of the story that the bones are telling. One could argue that in every translation lies the bias of the translator, and certainly in this case, the story being told has a particular agenda. However, the power of this tactic is that it specifically grounds itself in the perceived "unbiased" nature of science, along with its methods and protocols, clearly showing that certain anthropological facts cannot be contested. Moreover, by combining this framing with the agency and materialized voice of the remains with the embodied personal objects, we are provided with an example of how these processes are working together to facilitate a direct relationship between the visitors and the dead. The visitors are able to have a conversation of sorts where they can hear the story told by the remains, which the class leader can further explain and contextualize within the ARMH's reframing of the past.

In addition, the personal objects then embody both the lives and violent deaths of the victims. These findings thus nuance previous literature on the affective impact of objects on the public's relationship with the state (Cerulo 1993; Rose-Greenland 2014; Zubrzycki 2017) in that the objects are not producing feelings of nationalism or positive bonds. Rather, ARMH technicians are using the affective attachments produced by viewing these objects to challenge the state's sovereignty over collective memory and the shared responsibility for the violence, as the majority of the visitors believed that the violence demonstrated, or vocalized, by the graves was unwarranted and unjustified. As demonstrated in the last case, exhumations also had the power to create a mini truth and reconciliation experience for the children of both the perpetrators and the victims. These types of expressed sentiments are already a significant actualization of justice and seizing of state necropower. Furthermore, the majority of the visitors also agreed with the ARMH's "rights of the families" framing—that the families have the right to recover, identify, and rebury their loved ones, which directly contradicts the state's current relationship to its mass graves. Exhumations thus demonstrate the need for families to engage in these types of interventions.

In the next chapter, I analyze the role and impact of ARMH-led homage and reburial ceremonies for the recovered victims of the war and the regime. ARMH leaders argue that these events are the most important aspect of their work because they offer the families a long overdue chance to bury their loved ones in a respectful way that reflects the families' cultural and religious beliefs. I show that these events indeed provide families the forum to perform important death rituals. I also demonstrate that these events create a public space to 1) dignify and reincorporate the missing dead back into society; 2) display grief and suffering; 3) critique the state and make political demands; and 4) show how funerals and homage ceremonies are tangible forms of justice for victims' families.

4

REBURYING THE DEAD

Performance of Grief and Reframed Narratives

On November 20, 1975, the acting president of the Spanish government, Carlos Arias Navarro, declared, "Franco has died," ending Franco's almost forty-year regime and beginning three days of official mourning. At 12:30 a.m. on November 21, the archbishop of Madrid led a Catholic Mass attended by his family, the royal family, and government and military officials, all in full mourning dress. A military escort moved his body to the Salon de Columnas, where it lay in state for two days, allowing thousands of Spaniards to come and pay their respects. On November 22, Juan Carlos was crowned King of Spain, as Franco had declared him his successor in 1969 (Anon 1969).

On the morning of November 23, Franco's family had another private Mass before his body was ceremonially moved to the Plaza de Oriente, where a large stage had been erected. The coffin was draped in the Spanish flag alongside Franco's plumed dress hat, sword, and baton. On the main stage sat the newly crowned King and Queen, Franco's family, government and military leaders, and foreign dignitaries including Nelson Rockefeller, vice president of the United States, and Augusto Pinochet, the dictator of Chile at the time. The cardinal of Spain led another Mass, after which military officers moved the body to a motorized gun carrier located behind at least three tanks and the funeral party limos. Franco's funeral procession made its way through the streets of Madrid; the Royal Guard escorted the body, all on horseback and holding mounted flags, the effect reminiscent of a Roman color guard escorting a fallen emperor. Franco's procession finally made it to its final destination, the Valley of the Fallen. Over seventy thousand supporters and veterans of the war greeted the procession. Mourners, military officials, and government dignitaries filled the solemn mausoleum, and the site was blessed by the cardinal before Franco's body was finally buried at the base of the altar.[1]

Across sociological and anthropological literature the death of a human being provokes certain social and moral obligations, which are conveyed through culturally specific funeral practices (Hertz 2017; Robben 2017). Consequently, what a society does with its dead is illustrative of the stratification of the citizenry within the social order (Robben 2017). This can be most clearly demonstrated by looking at how societies glorify their political, cultural, and religious leaders when they bury them, in comparison to how they treat their indigent or criminal dead. The differences between these groups reflect important, societally prescribed ideas of the importance of that person's life.

As described above, Franco received all possible social and religious death rituals, a stark contrast to his hundreds of thousands victims who lie in unmarked graves littering the Spanish countryside—many purposely buried without religious rituals or respect and interred facedown in unconsecrated ground. Franco's regime, and the Catholic Church, systematically denied the families of these victims the right to rebury or publicly mourn their dead under penalty of violence or death. The democratic transition maintained this official negation of the dead. As such, the state rendered these dead invisible by insisting they had no rights or religious, societal, or political meaning.

As has been extensively discussed in earlier chapters, forensics-based human rights groups have fought against this negation and have resurrected the missing back to their loved ones and society through scientific exhumations. Scholars of human rights have argued that this process is necessary for survivors to have closure, the dead to undergo important death rituals, and the continuation of a healthy politic (Robben 2000). Accordingly, for survivors to have closure and to reincorporate the recovered back into society, the dead must go through a series of rituals, such as reburials or homage events.

The return and reincorporation of the dead via exhumations creates complex sociocultural events within towns that have suffered violence (Azevedo 2016). In Spain, unlike other more recent examples of violence in Latin America or the Balkans, there are few direct survivors or perpetrators of the violence still alive; mostly grandchildren are behind exhumation efforts. As such, the complexity of these events in Spain has more to do with dignifying the dead as being worthy of revered remembrance, reincorporating them back into the citizenry and reclaiming the families' dignity, all important forms of post-transitional justice.

The process of dignifying and reincorporating the dead begins with establishing their identities, thereby ending the uncertainty of their "missing' " status. Once an identity is objectively associated with remains, the victim can then be reintegrated back into society as a recognized member (Duterme 2016: 7–8). Reassociating the dead with their names reaffirms their existence—a triumph over the perpetrators' efforts to obliterate their victims and a triumph over the state's negation of them (Duterme 2016: 7–8). ARMH reburials and homage events thus serve to both reincorporate the recovered dead back into society and provide another platform for the ARMH's reframed narrative of the past.

In this chapter, I focus on the role and impact of ARMH-led homage and reburial events for recovered victims of the war and the regime. ARMH leaders maintain that reburial and homage ceremonies are the most important aspect of their work because the ceremonies finally offer the families a chance to bury their loved ones in a respectful way that reflects their cultural and religious beliefs. Though these events provide families the opportunity to perform important death rituals, they also create a public space to carry out overdue death rituals, including religious death rites, express their grief, and critique the state. Additionally, homage and reburial events also create the opportunity to achieve an important reparative justice, as they dignify and reincorporate the missing dead back into society. This chapter, however, also complicates the argument that identified remains are always necessary for the dignification and reincorporation of the dead. In the instances of unidentified remains, depending on the town and the situation, the recovered remains can embody the collective dignification of *all* of the town's missing.

REINCORPORATING AND DIGNIFYING THE IDENTIFIED MISSING

After the ARMH has recovered and identified a body, the next steps involve honoring and reburying the dead. The ARMH always offers to provide an homage ceremony, and many families accept it. Although homage events vary in how and where they are performed, most follow a specific routine that begins with an official statement, or performance that is open to the public, whether it takes place in a town hall or a community theater.

The events often include public statements about the violence that occurred, the technical work done to retrieve the remains, and sometimes a statement from the relatives of the victims about what it means to them to have their loved ones back. After the homage, the body (or bodies, depending on the situation) is reburied. On rare occasions, there is a Catholic Mass and then the actual reburial. The association also helps provide a receptacle for the remains and a headstone if needed.

Activists, through homage and reburial ceremonies, have another platform to expose local communities to their counternarrative of the violence of the war, the regime, and the symbolic violence of the democratic transition. However, unlike technical work, these events do not rely as heavily on the depoliticized science approach; rather, they focus on the emotive and personal details of the dead and their living relatives. This is not to say that the science is entirely missing; the depoliticized science that led to finding and identifying the remains is noted at key moments. According to the leaders of the ARMH, they are only there to offer help to the families so that they can have the kind of ceremony they want. The ARMH thereby places the responsibility for any voiced political claims or arguments during these events on the family and invited performers—not on the association's technical side.

However, as with other memory events, homage and reburial ceremonies do offer a platform for the political wing of the ARMH to make more explicit political statements and demands. As previously discussed, the ARMH has two different wings within its organization. The first is the technical and scientific side, which attempts to stay as depoliticized as possible to protect the perceived unbiased nature of their technical interventions. The technical side is much more prevalent during the scientific excavations and exhumations. They also usually play a small pedagogical role in homage ceremonies, with the lead archeologist often giving a quick review of the work done to find, exhume, and identify the remains.

The other wing of the ARMH is explicitly political and engages in making and negotiating political demands. The president and the vice president, as well as the staff who run the social media accounts, mostly do this work. As many homage and reburial events are public, the political wing often participates, either directly in the event or in a separate press conference. During these speeches, which can be considered calls for legal justice, the political side often denounces the violence of the past and the silencing that occurred during the democratic transition, pointing out the failures of the centralized state to address the past in a meaningful way. However, the ARMH does not associate with a particular political party and always reaffirms their advocacy as being on the side of the families of the victims and the families' rights to access the technical and identifying science.

Villafranca

An example of an homage and reburial ceremony that illustrates the power of these events occurred in Villafranca del Bierzo, a small town in the Galician region of Spain. Villafranca, which sits within a narrow valley surrounded by beautiful green mountains, is known for its summer music festivals. Stone-faced churches and buildings line the town's cobblestone roads. On the main roadway, a community theater sits next to the town hall. Across the street are restaurants with open-air seating that cater to tourists.

The homage event that occurred at this theater in August 2016 was for all the victims of repression (over sixty) of the citizens of

Villafranca del Bierzo. However, the event was specifically for two recently recovered victims, executed by the government in October 1948, who were to be reburied after the event. They were a mother (Vicenta) and son (Jesús) who lost their lives for housing armed guerrilla fighters who had killed a Civil Guard during an encounter earlier that month. The Civil Guard's retribution was swift and brutal. The mother's death orphaned her remaining six children. Government officials buried the mother and son together, without caskets or grave markers, between other graves in the cemetery. Vicenta's brother, Vicente, had died in the Mauthausen death camp, where the Franco regime had sent him as punishment for fighting on the Republican side. He perished before the United States Army liberated the camp in May 1945.

One of Vicenta's remaining children, Milagros, contacted the association in 2014, and the exhumation occurred in October 2015. In this case, as soon as the forensic archeologist could determine the sex of the remains, it was possible to identify the bodies. However, a volunteer forensic anthropologist did a full examination of the remains, signed off on the official identifications, and wrote a full report. After this was completed, Milagros, the association, and the local mayor organized the homage event. However, as Milagros is a religious woman, she wanted a Catholic Mass for her brother and mother before the reburial. The mayor had to arrange it, as the priest was initially not interested in providing one for "Reds," illustrating the long-lasting division within the Spanish Catholic Church.

Press Coverage of the Event

Language and framing, as many experts have shown (Benford and Snow 2000; Goffman 1974; Snow and Benford 1988), have an important impact on how people understand their social world. Hence, it is sociologically important to analyze how the press covers events such as these. With this in mind, I did a content analysis of twenty-one news articles covering both the announcement of the event and the event itself.

In the sample of ten announcement articles of Vicenta and Jesús's homage and reburial, all included a brief historical overview of the violence. Each specified that the state police had killed the two victims in 1948 during an implementation of the unofficial "law of escape" (which allowed state officials to shoot "escaping" prisoners) and that the ARMH had exhumed the victims in October 2015.[2] In the historical retelling of their deaths, I expected to see the word *executed*. Though the regime never formalized the law, technically making these kinds of killings illegal, the state fully supported them. However, eight of the articles used the word *asesinados*, (assassinated or murdered) when describing the deaths of Vicenta and Jesús. The other two articles more euphemistically stated that the two victims had died during an "application" of the law. However, one of those articles also later used the word *assassinated*.

Linguistically, the use of the word *asesinados* is interesting, making it seem like the writers were suggesting that Vicenta and Jesús were not killed through judicial means. Additionally, the word was often coupled with contextualizing sentences to further reinforce the idea that these deaths were murders and not legal executions. For example, an article from *La Marea* features the title "The ARMH Returns the Remains of Two Murdered by Francoism to Their Relatives in an Event in Villafranca del Bierzo." Again, linguistic choices matter; something as simple as using the word *assassinated* or *murdered* rather than *executed*, or the ambiguous death by application of a law, changes the story of the lives and deaths of the two victims. Depending on which word is used, Vicenta and Jesús go from being two dangerous communist guerrilla warriors executed while escaping justice to two repression victims murdered by an unjust state.

As the ARMH always puts out a press release about its work, I also compared it with my news sample. All of the announcement articles either directly quoted the ARMH's official statement or paraphrased it. Interestingly, albeit not surprisingly, the original use of *asesinados* was in the ARMH report. As such, this is a direct example of how the ARMH strategically introduces its reframed narrative of the past violence into the mainstream via the press who then amplifies that narrative to the meso level of society.

Additionally, it also shows how the ARMH tactically actualizes the social change its movement hopes to create, through press releases that strategically and linguistically reframe the past. Not all of the journalists used the exact language, yet nine of the ten announcement articles either led with or eventually used the word *asesinados*. The announcement articles also served to reinforce the rights of families frame that roots much of the ARMH's forensics-based human rights claims. For example, the announcement articles in the newspaper *Hipertextual* reminded readers that the event was also to "remember the more than 114,000 victims of forced disappearance, which has converted Spain into the second country in the world with disappearances after Cambodia. Under the water dams, in the ditches along freeways, and off cliffs, thousands of people continue today buried and forgotten by democracy. Victims like Vicenta and Jesús only want to be reclaimed and buried with dignity and that they can one day enjoy the rights and liberties they were robbed of." Again, the violence and the political dynamics of the violence are mentioned, yet the article focuses more on the needs and rights of the dead, which are to be reunited with their families and reburied with dignity. Additionally, it associates the recovered dead with the recovery of democracy and liberties.

In a formal interview, Hernan, a man in his seventies, also connected the previous political lives of the dead to recovery efforts: "These people paid taxes when they were alive. They were our citizens and they participated in democracy. Now the government should pay to find them." For Hernan and the writer of the article, there is a lingering sense that the victims of the violence, who were once citizens of a democracy, should be supported by the contemporary government so that their families can receive rights and liberties that they have long been denied.

Historical Memory and Dignification

Seven of the ten announcement articles also made note of Vicenta's brother, Vicente, and his death at Mauthausen. I posit that including that information not only highlights the family's compounded tragedies but also reminds readers that Franco's regime sent thousands of Spaniards to die in Nazi concentration camps. The inclusion of that information supports another goal of the ARMH and the historical memory movement, which is for Spanish society to know a more accurate and complete history of its violent past.

In addition to reminding readers of a forgotten or ignored history, the news articles also began an important aspect of dignifying and reincorporating the victims at the meso level by including their photos. Six of the announcement articles included a portrait of Vicenta as a smiling young woman in sepia tones. If one did not know better, the articles could have passed as obituaries. Her portrait concretized both her story and the horror of state terror.

Depoliticized Science Framing

The initial coverage of the science behind the coming event was basic. However, a *Hipertextual* follow-up to the exhumation coverage was located in the science section of the newspaper and titled "The Dead of Kilometer 411 Return from Oblivion." The focus of the article was on the science and research behind the ARMH's intervention into solving Milagros's case. Interspersed with descriptions of the historical and scientific research and techniques was direct political commentary and implied criticism of the centralized state's handling of discussions of the past violence. For example, the article included these lines: "The historic, forensic, and anthropological study permitted the identification of the bodies of Vicenta and Jesús. Even so, they took DNA samples in case one day 'Justice' wants to investigate their case." The suggestion was that although DNA was not necessary to identify the bodies, as forensic anthropology techniques were able to do so, the DNA may one day be able to bring legal justice if the state decides to pursue it. The amnesty laws make this currently impossible, yet the article suggests to readers that the courts should investigate these criminal acts.

The article went on to describe the coming event, pointing out that it would take place next to the building where, eighty years before, the municipality had been taken over by the rebels. The end of the article quotes the vice president of the ARMH: "Democracy is paralyzed, so the event on that day will have a special symbolic charge and will be very emotional," as "Milagros has always wanted a place to leave flowers [for her dead]."

I suggest that the majority of the scientific coverage fits directly into the ARMH's self-framing as being the depoliticized and scientifically motivated association that acts as the medium for long-grieving families who want to rebury their loved ones. Across the articles, no commentary on the ARMH's work suggests that the association is anything other than the group that recovered, identified, and will be helping to rebury the two victims' bodies. However, the event, is seen as tied to larger conversations about the Spanish state's memory politics.

THE EVENT

The homage for the victims of repression took place in the community theater of the town. The theater is large, seating at least 150 people. The stage is small but has an ornate white façade that wraps around and above the main stage. Before the event began, attendees and the local press gathered on the sidewalk. The press mostly interviewed the victims' families about what it was like to be there, as well as Emilio Silva, the president of the ARMH. His grandfather had been a resident of the town before the rebels arrested him along with twelve others; they were killed and buried in a mass grave.

Once the doors opened, the theater began to fill rapidly. It soon became clear that there was not enough seating for everyone; in the end, some attendees had to stand in the back and along the sides of the theater.

The homage began when two ARMH members brought in the small caskets. The entire audience applauded while the team members climbed the stairs and placed the caskets on a small table at the front of the stage. Sitting at a long table next to it was the town's entire city council, including the mayor. Leaders of the ARMH, including its president, Emilio Silve, then welcomed the audience to the homage ceremony.

The mayor, a member of the People's Party (Partido Popular), spoke about the importance of remembering the violence

FIGURE 4.1 Theater and the beginning of homage event

FIGURE 4.2 View from stage during homage event

of the past instead of silencing it. He highlighted the power of exhumations: "[The family] has been able to locate and recover the remains, as well as put up a plaque in that space to remember what happened there. The families now have the ability to accompany the remains and bury them in the municipal cemetery. We hope that what happened in those years, that this kind of repression, is never repeated. That brothers, friends, and people in general never, NEVER take up arms to solve their ideological differences. To do this, we must remember all of the victims of persecution, torture, and murder." He spoke articulately and movingly, recalling that the person who held his job in 1936 was murdered and thrown into a ditch. Interestingly, the murdered mayor's family was also in attendance. After pronouncing, "Never Again," the mayor stood up and grabbed the two bouquets of lilies sitting on the table in front of him, went over to the small caskets, placed the flowers on top of them, and held a very long moment of silence. The people I was standing next to, somewhat jokingly, remarked that he was definitely going to lose his next election for being so supportive of the "Reds." Others later commented that the mayor's actions "were a shock" and were promising for future reconciliation goals.[3]

In many ways, the mayor's speech and actions epitomized what it means for a community to perform reparative justice through the reincorporation of the recovered dead back into the citizenry of both the town and the country. The mayor, through his discourse and actions, publicly declared that Vicenta and Jesús had actually been victims of state terror and not criminals deserving of their deaths.[4] Furthermore, he unequivocally denounced the long silence imposed by the state and attempted to give revered remembrance to the victims and their family.

In his speech, the mayor also emphatically endorsed the ARMH's counter-memory of the violence, which is that violence

FIGURE 4.3 Audience watches homage event

of the war and regime were unjust and that the historical record suggesting otherwise is false. The city council, through their presence and silence, seemed to be condoning the mayor's perspective and approach to the past. At the very least, the city council became complicit in the mayor's actions. This aspect of the homage holds a tremendous amount of symbolic importance for the legitimacy of the ARMH, the counter-memory it presents, and the actualization of new forms of justice, especially because the mayor was associated with the ruling party at the time, who have been, and remain, obstructionist concerning any transitional justice efforts.

The homage continued with readings and presentations by team leaders including the forensic archeologist, the president of

the association, and the association's secretary. The archeologist's
speech focused on how the ARMH conducts its technical work.
He reviewed how the team follows UN protocols on mass grave
exhumations, which follow precise, objective, and scientifically
grounded steps. He continued by explaining that the workers
follow this particular protocol, rather than just the humanitarian protocol to recover the remains, in case one day their work
is used in criminal proceedings investigating the past violence.
His review of the protocols assumed that the audience would
be receptive to the idea that science is objective and untainted
by political belief. He continued, explaining that through the
use of scientific exhumations the bones are then able to speak
their own objective truths, which is why they are so powerful
and important—not just for the victims' families but for all of
Spain. The archeologist's speech then focused on the challenges
that the ARMH faces while conducting this work, including the
lack of state support, lack of a national DNA database, and the
resounding fear that remains in rural Spain.

The archeologist, after finishing his speech, invited Milagros
to the podium and handed her the forensic report. That hand-
ing off served to symbolize, much like a birth or death certifi-
cate, the end of the identification process. These two individuals
were now officially and publicly recognized, both by the state
(the mayor and city council) and by scientific study (the forensic report); they had been officially and scientifically identified,
and their remains were reassociated with their names. In this
moment, one of the key promises of forensics-based human
rights had been fulfilled.

Although the science was not the primary focus of the event,
the audience was reminded that those being reburied that day
had been found, exhumed, and identified via scientific and historical methods, highlighting the importance of the science to

the larger historical memory movement and to the dignifying of the recovered dead.

After the handoff of the forensic reports, a renowned poet, Juan Carlos Mestre, gave a rousing reading of "Tailor's Daughter," a poem dedicated to those who suffered from repression in the town. The poetry reading was intense and theatrical. Mestre was captivating, at times pausing to look directly at the family of the victims. His poem told a story about the anniversary of the coup d'état in 1936, comets flying through space, the passing of time, the fear that leads to silence, and little stories about those who had been killed by the fascists. Near the end he read, "Sixty-four years after the fascist uprising, the grandson of Emilio Silva . . . will find his grandfather's grave in a ditch at the entrance of a town. . . . According to the gospel of Nathan Zach, when God said for the first time, 'Let there be light,' what he meant to say was that he didn't want to be in the darkness any longer." When he finished, he went over to Milagros and gave her a hug and kiss on the cheek. She, like many others, was crying.

The last speaker was Milagros, the daughter and sister of the victims. She began by saying, "With this act, I can finally close the pain that I have been facing for more than sixty years. . . . I have dreamed thousands of times of this moment, and finally, I can make my loved ones rest in peace." She thanked the association for finding her mother and brother. She also thanked the mayor for being there, acknowledging her family, and helping to organize the event. She thanked her "new family" of the historical memory movement for also supporting her. Then she said that she was going to read a letter she had written to her mother:

My dearest mother, you live in the corners of my heart. You have never left me. I am waiting to give you and my brother a hug. You were never killed in our hearts. When they hurt us, it is because they do not have a mother. When they are cold to us, it is because they do not have a mother. . . . Oh dearest mother, how much I needed you. How much I have dreamed with you. I look at the moon and think of you. I see the roundness of the moon and think of you, of your face. I remember all things, the socks you made. How could I remember all these things with only ten years of age? It has cost me a lot to remember you, mom. I talk with the moon and tell her how much I want to see you. And yet, how happy I am knowing that I am not alone, because you are always by my side.

When she finished her letter, the crowd applauded loudly.

The final act of the homage ceremony began when the ARMH historian and Milagros's daughter carried the caskets out of the theater. As they walked out, music filled the theater, and the audience rose to its feet, applauding and singing along to "Canto a Libertad Labordeta."[5] The lyrics speak of those who have been fighting for freedom that has yet to be achieved, as well as how those who survive the battle have to keep fighting for those who have fallen. The chorus sings, "There will be a day, when we will look up and see a land that is free." It is a very moving and emotive song, especially when sung by over 150 people. During the song, people raised their arms in the one-fisted Republican salute, others waved the Republican flag, and some simply yelled "Viva la República!" Other victims' families in the audience stood, sang, applauded, and cried as they watched the small coffins leave the theater.

The song, in the context of an homage and reburial event, was not only an opportunity to participate and voice shared grief with the family burying their loved ones but also with the other families in attendance still searching for their relatives. The audience, in singing along, were engaging in a collective and almost religious act of collective grief. Yet unlike singing a hymn at a

religious funeral, the audience was not singing about the promise of heaven and a loving God. Rather, they were lifting up
their voices in the secular and political hope that tomorrow will
bring justice and freedom. Considering that many in the audience were relatives of the undiscovered disappeared, the moment
also symbolized, as one person told me, the hope "that one day
maybe they too could find their missing relatives and bury them
with dignity like those being buried [after the ceremony]."

From the theater, the audience and the family walked the
remains up to the church on the top of the hill where the cemetery was located. Carlos Mestre and I were the only two associated with the ARMH who attended the Mass. The rest of
the ARMH, as well as all the people who came to the homage,
waited outside the church. This was not meant to be disrespect-
ful per se; it was more of a reflection that many associated with
the historical memory movement still hold resentment against
the Catholic Church's role and complicity in both the violence and with the regime. The priest presiding over the funeral
did not seem particularly thrilled to be officiating. He led an
extremely mundane, borderline hostile, service, saying things
like "I presume they were nice enough people. However, I did
not know them. Either way, they were both children of God,
I suppose." He did not go out of his way to be warm or even particularly understanding of the events that led to the premature
deaths of those receiving the final sacrament. Although it was
clear that he was uncomfortable, the priest still performed his
ecclesiastical role, and that was all the family had desired: that
their loved ones receive a Catholic funeral. However, the priest
declined to go to the graveyard to bless the grave, citing stomach
pains. He pointed out that it was unnecessary for him to go as
the cemetery was already consecrated ground and did not need
any additional blessings.

FIGURE 4.4 A relative and cemetery worker rebury the dead

After the mass, the extended family of the victims carried the flowers and the remains to the gravesite. The crowd waiting outside the church followed behind. Once we arrived at the gravesite, ironically in the same cemetery the victims had originally been buried, the remains were passed off to a cemetery worker standing in the official grave. Once the remains were in the ground, the family threw flowers into the grave one by one. Afterward, the male ARMH team members took turns burying the caskets. When the graves were covered, the vice president affixed a black marble grave marker on top of the grave.

Once the reburial was finished, everyone walked back down to the town center to drive to the restaurant where more than forty mourners enjoyed a multicourse meal. At the end of the dinner, Milagros gave a speech thanking the association for its work and specifically for finding her mother after all these years. She remarked that in many ways, the association had become like another family to her and one that she will be forever indebted.

Press Coverage of the Homage and Reburial of Vicenta and Jesús

As with the announcement articles, coverage of the actual event varied in the description of the two victims' deaths. In the sample of eleven news articles covering the event, six used the word *assassinated*, three used *executed*, and one used both the words *paseado*, which literally means "went for a walk," but is a common euphemism for those people who are extrajudicially killed, and *fusilado*, meaning "shot to death." This article, I posit, was using the more common Spanish vernacular to describe the victims, as opposed to making specific linguistic distinctions suggestive as to whether or not the violence was justified or not. There was also coverage by an American university paper that used the word *disappeared* to describe the deaths, linguistically connecting the Spanish movement to that of Argentina and the Southern Cone. As with the announcement articles, though, the majority of the coverage of the event articles, when discussing the historical aspects of the story, relied on the ARMH's press release before the event.

As for the three articles that used the word *executed*, the rest of the coverage was more sympathetic toward the plight of the family. All three noted the failure of the Spanish state to appropriately deal with the past violence and either quoted or followed the language of the ARMH's press release, which framed the violence as unjust state terror. A key example of this was an article from *Diario de León* in which the author plays with the meaning of words to describe the deaths of Vicenta and Jesús. It stated, "Both executed judicially—if there were ever a time to use the word justice in a meaningless way it is here—in retaliation from the dictatorship for an armed confrontation that occurred in their hometown, Castañerias, in October 1948." Though the article used the word *ajusticiados*, a synonym for legally executed, and clever Spanish wordplay, the author goes further by clarifying that "justice" was never part of this story.

Testimonies of Violence and Dignification of the Dead

One of the most important aspects of transitional justice is the victims' ability to feel heard (Herman 2015; Nauenberg 2015). As discussed in chapter 1, Spain has never had any real transitional justice or truth commissions; this role often devolves into smaller local events. In this case, I argue that the news coverage of the homage and reburial event acts as a similar platform, albeit bigger than the microinteractions of chapter 1 and smaller than actual truth commissions. In this case, the local news media were the transmitting sources for the meso-level dignification and reincorporation of the dead, as well as giving a platform for Milagros's testimony about the impact of the violence and her grief.

For example, an *El Diario* article covering the event placed the portrait of Vicenta next to a quote from Milagros: "Do you remember a television series that described the suffering of black slaves in America? Well, my brother Eduardo returned home with his back full of lashes like those of Kunta Kinte, the protagonist of that series; his feet burned with matches. . . . I was the one who healed all those wounds and burns." Milagros, in this quote, is primarily testifying about her family's experience with state terror and torture. She then goes on to connect that testimony to a historical injustice and a popular television show (*Roots*) that dramatized that violence. Milagros, in her interview, continued giving witness to her family's pain, explaining that the state had also incarcerated another brother for over six months, and when he returned, he was so traumatized that he could not speak about his experiences. He also refused to consider searching for his mother and brother because of the trauma he suffered. It was only after his death that Milagros began her search for her mother and brother.

Another article, "The Memory of the Earth Took the Floor," led with a large photograph of the two ARMH members bringing in the two caskets to the stage while those in attendance applauded. Milagros and her family, front and center, were dressed in white. The title of the article is telling, as it suggests that those pulled from the ground, the earth's memory, are publicly speaking. The article quotes Milagros: "I have found my mother and I am not going to cry." She then explains that the emotionality of being at her mother and brother's long-overdue funeral engulfed her as the caskets rose to the stage.

All of the articles reinforced that the event was not only for the two victims but was also a ceremony to honor all the repression victims of the town. One article stated the event honored the "over sixty citizens who were assassinated, and the many more deported to the extermination camp Mauthausen in a municipality of Villafranca where there was no warfare." This type of news coverage reminded the readers that this region was never a battlefield and yet at least sixty people were murdered for their political beliefs and even more were sent to die in Nazi death camps. As such, these news stories amplified historical truths often ignored by an official accounting of the past.

The event coverage also provided Milagros the opportunity to publicly express criticism of the Spanish government and its continued disparagement of the victims. In one article, she is quoted as saying, "I will write to the president of the government and say, 'I have finally found them.' I will also send Rajoy a newspaper article with news of the funeral and a letter where I will ask him why he has a person like Rafael Hernando at his side; a person who says atrocities, like we [the victims' families] only worry about our dead when there are subsidies." Milagros, in this quote, is vocalizing her triumph over a state that wanted to keep her mother and brother confined to oblivion in a clandestine grave. She is also demonstrating defiance to the fear that plagued her family, as she plans to send a letter directly to the head of state to show him how unafraid and angry she is at the continued denigration of the victims and their families.

As all eleven articles covering the ceremony had a sympathetic tone, one could argue that at the very least, the intense shaming of the defeated at least ended at the local media level. The human-interest story of an older woman who waited and fought for sixty years to find and rebury her mother and brother in a dignified way is perhaps a much more compelling story. Either way, the compassionate coverage puts the centralized state's belittling of the victims' families, such as suggesting that they are only interested in recovering their loved ones for government subsidies, in a jarring juxtaposition, including the actions of the mayor. In the coverage from InfoBierzo, there were four photos of the mayor and city council, two specifically just of the mayor bringing the flowers over to the caskets and holding his minute of silence in from of them. Again, the importance of the city's mayor, a member of the right-wing party, fully participating and honoring the dead cannot be understated, especially in comparison to the quotes of his fellow party members.

In addition to providing critiques of the state, the coverage also offered another chance for the ARMH leadership to argue for the breaking of the repressive silence of the past. In the *Yale Globalist*, as well as at least three other articles, Emilio Silva is quoted: "I hope that acts like this one help the people to speak." As with the ARMH's other performative actions, such as excavations and exhumations, homage and reburial ceremonies provide a platform to actualize the breaking of the silence that still permeates Spanish society, especially in smaller rural communities. The local news coverage of the ARMH's homage and reburial ceremonies adds another layer to this actualization of breaking the silence. Furthermore, this coverage, can be seen as a form of transitional justice in that it pushes Spanish towns to acknowledge their shared past of violence and the rights of the victims' families.

In this case, the homage and reburial ceremony of Vicenta and Jesús, as well as the press coverage of the event, achieved many of the key goals of forensics-based human rights. The dead were publicly reassociated with their identities, they were officially reincorporated and dignified as revered citizens by the local government (not as undeserving criminal communists), and the family was able to participate in long-overdue rituals, display their grief, share their testimony of violence, and critique the state.

In Spain, unlike other postconflict or postauthoritarian situations, direct descendants of the victims are not entitled to government restitution or even a truth commission. Homage and reburial events, like the one for Vicenta and Jesús, are thus immeasurably important and a true form of achieved and reparative justice. Having the city council and mayor present, and the corresponding local news coverage, is probably as close as the family will ever get to receiving state recognition and accountability for their suffering.

Moreover, the mayor's full embrace of the ARMH's reframing of the narrative of violence represents a symbolic and tangible victory for the ARMH and the families. Although this victory of seizing and successfully reframing the state's necropower over the historical narrative did not occur at the macro level, it did happen in a region that historically was a stronghold of Francoism and is still heavily conservative. Again, while the impact may have been more acute at the local level, like a stone thrown into a pond there are ripple effects that have yet to arrive.

Importantly, the homage and reburial ceremony for Vicenta and Jesús, and the subsequent news coverage, allowed for a very public critique of the state's necropolitics. The ceremony, although focused on the unjust and untimely murders of the two victims at the hands of the state, also emphasized the remembrance of all those who suffered from repression in the region. All of the speakers, including the mayor, spoke of the centralized state's failings to address the past, including how this state-sanctioned silencing has perpetuated the suffering of the victims' families. The event, as well as the quotes from ARMH's leaders in the news coverage, was also very much a rallying call for further political mobilization and the breaking of the repressive silencing of the past.

HOMAGE AND DIGNIFICATION OF THE UNIDENTIFIED

However, not all homage and reburial ceremonies take place in the presence of identified remains. This would seem to run counter to the promise of the forensics-based human rights movement and of science's ability to restore the identities of the dead. Yet, it is not always possible to identify the remains due to the quality or deterioration of the bones, the lack of a comprehensive DNA database for victims, or a combination of these two.

In some cases, the bones are too damaged because of the acidity or humidity in the ground to use DNA testing. Though it is not the desired outcome, some towns decide to hold an homage and reburial ceremony anyway.

An example of this occurred with the remains of nine men the ARMH exhumed near the town of Valderas, just outside the city of León. The exhumation occurred in 2012, but the ARMH could only run DNA testing in 2015, thanks to the help of the Argentine Forensic Anthropology Team (EAAF). When the EAAF ran the tests, it compared the remains with the living relatives of the missing, but it could not identify a single body due to a combination of poorly conserved remains and human error. In spite of not being able to identify the bones, however, the victims' families decided to proceed with a reburial and homage ceremony. The official homage and reburial was split across three separate formal events.

Town Memory Events

The day's events began in the town lecture hall. The local historian and memory activist gave a detailed presentation about the violence of the village and the surrounding areas. He spoke about who the victims were, how they died, and how the violence irrevocably changed the history of the town.

The ARMH's lead archeologist then gave a technical presentation to help further educate the town on the work that was done. He reviewed how the ARMH investigates each case, starting with the victims' families asking the ARMH to find their loved ones, the historical research that is conducted, and then a quick review of the technical process of searching for and exhuming the graves. This speech also explored various challenges, such as changes in the land, lack of state support or a national DNA database, and the fear that still silences the voices of many Spaniards living in small villages.

The archeologist then explained to the town that none of the bodies exhumed in 2012 had been successfully identified in the original DNA testing.[6] He asked any relatives of the victims to come to the designated area to redo DNA swabs for another round of testing. While the actual execution of this process was chaotic due to a lack of organization on the association's part, eventually the team was able to obtain samples from everyone. Unfortunately, the second round of DNA testing also proved to be inconclusive, and the nine bodies will never be officially identified unless the science improves.

After the presentations were over, the official homage event began with the vice president of the ARMH holding a press conference at the town hall. The room was so crowded that many people stood along the walls or in the hallway. Members and volunteers of the association and some relatives of the dead brought in plastic boxes containing the remains of the missing. As they entered the hall, everyone waiting inside stood up and began applauding fervently. Like the homage ceremony for Vicenta and Jesús, this was the first time that the remains were recognized as reincorporated citizens deserving of revered respect in death. As the boxes entered the hall, the living transformed the long-missing dead to the nameless, yet still important, recovered citizenry of the town.

The vice president, the first to speak, commended the victims for fighting for their beliefs in democracy. He also said the killings should be addressed by the centralized Spanish state in the pursuit of legal justice for the victims and their families. At one point, he referenced the painting pasted on the side of each box containing the remains when he said, "They were not burying

FIGURE 4.5 Town hall reception before reburial event

bodies, they were burying seeds." The painting depicts a group of men burying two others killed by rebel troops. The imagery of burying seeds suggests that the bodies will not just disappear in the ground but will grow into a new life of resistance, which is a very common refrain in the movement.

After the speeches at the town hall had ended, a woman approached the remains, wanting to touch the boxes. When she got closer, she realized that there was no identifying name on each box. She asked the vice president, "Where are the names? How do you know who is who?" He responded, "They are not identified. We could not get a conclusive DNA identification on any of them." She nodded slowly, looking disappointed but said, "It's been a long time." He said, trying to give her a glimmer of hope, that the bodies "could, maybe, one day be identified if the technology got better." He explained that each box contained a sealed bone sample for future testing, just in case.

Secular Funeral for the Unidentified Dead

The ARMH then transported the remains closer to the cemetery's entrance and activists handed the plastic boxes to family members to bring into the graveyard. The cemetery, about the size of a soccer field, was located on top of a small hill overlooking the Spanish countryside, which was full of yellow wheat and red poppies. The communal tomb was located in the middle of the graveyard and had many red, yellow, and purple Republican flags decorating the site. The tomb was the central focus of the ceremony.

During the reburial ceremony, many of the victims' family members gave speeches reinforcing the analogy of burying seeds, as well as the idea that the earth holds more than just memories. One such speech said how exhumations help to recover not just the dead themselves but also their identity and dignity. He also went on to say that after almost eighty years, nine of the town's seventy-seven missing were finally home. He ended his speech by demanding that we never forget what happened. Later, another man, a son of one of the victims, talked about the searing loss of his father. He ended his speech, a hand resting on one of the boxes, with "Father, rest in peace, your son does not forget you." Even though he did not know if one of the nine recovered remains was actually his father, he was still able to give him a eulogy. In some ways, not having the identities confirmed allowed all of the victims' families to participate in the reburial as though they were commemorating their lost loved ones, and there was no way to say they were not actually doing so.

After the speeches, two teenagers played the song "Bones."[7] The song starts with the lyrics "They could be, at first glance, only bones, ramshackle bones buried at the edge of the road." The song continues, saying that the bones are, in fact, evidence of a story, "a desperate, exhausted history of premeditated terror" that can only be told by the bones themselves. The bones need to be brought to the "pure air of the living," as they are waiting to be hugged, kissed, and given a real goodbye. The song, like many of the funerary speeches that day, reinforced the idea that the bones were embodied with the humanity of the people who once inhabited them, including the desire for vindication and the tender care of their families who have been searching for them. Furthermore, this kind of rhetoric highlights the concept that the dead retain an emotional connection with the living and that the living have a continued responsibility to find and care for their dead (see Kligman 1988). The focus is on the bones, which, of course, can only be found through the process of exhumation. Exhumations are thus the instrument through which the bones of the dead can be brought back "to the pure air, so they can live" again.

Later two female relatives, both prominent activists, read every single name of the dead from the town and their personal descriptions, such as age, occupation, whether they were married or had children, their political affiliation, whether they had been tortured, and how they were killed. After each name and personal history, they rang a bell. The remaining speeches focused on the nine remains, as being symbolic of the entire seventy-seven. As these families had waited almost eighty years to

FIGURE 4.6 Relatives of the victims view newly placed headstone

participate in a public death ritual, it seemed less important that the bodies were identified than it was to have a reburial. In this respect, the importance of restituting the identities of the disappeared was ostensibly less important than having a collective rite of mourning.

After almost two hours of speeches, musical interludes, and the planting of two trees on either side of the tomb—again to symbolize the seeds and vitality of the dead—the remains were placed in the mausoleum,[8] and it was covered with a large black marble slab inscribed with all the names of the disappeared and the phrase "Only the forgotten are dead; your ultimate wish is to be remembered." The crowd yelled "Viva!" and had a "family" photo taken of all of the relatives in front of the tomb. Unlike the reburial of Vicenta and Jesús, the town had decided to rebury their dead without any religious death rites.

Conclusion

In this case, as with the previous reinterment ceremony, the ARMH was able to present historical and technical accounts of its work to reinforce a reframed memory of the past. This reframing portrayed the violence and repression of the war and the regime as being both unjust and an attack on innocent civilians and human rights. Furthermore, it reframed transition-era politics that maintained a petrified silence and gave amnesty to perpetrators as being a continuation of Francoism, which perpetuated the suffering of the victims.

Although dignification often refers to identified remains, in the case of these unidentified remains, I posit that a process of dignification and justice still occurred. The ceremony included eulogies for specific members of the deceased by their relatives.

The relatives read each of the names of the dead as though they were buried that day. The symbolic dignification of all of the missing was the more important aspect of this reburial ceremony. The uttering of a name, especially when couched within public death rituals, reaffirms the presence of the person and emphasizes the individual, as well as the impact of his or her loss. As there are still sixty-eight citizens missing from the town that have yet to be found and exhumed, it is possible that future forensic work will one day discover the remaining bodies and lead to identifications and future reburial ceremonies.

Like the homage and reburial ceremony for Vicenta and Jesús, the reburial of the unidentified provided a public space for the collective expression of grief, not only for the direct family members but also for the town as a whole. Whether they were relatives of the missing or not, people came to see the memory events and to witness their former neighbors' funerals. The importance of having witnesses to the public display of grief should not be underestimated. Additionally, this event provided a platform for victims and their families to give personal testimonies of violence centered on their perspective of the events, as opposed to the perpetrators. The families were also able to display their grief and publicly perform long-awaited death rituals, which speaks to the enduring and perpetual torture that enforced disappearance creates. Perhaps the deep emotionality of publicly expressed long-lasting grief is what makes these events resonant and powerful.

In Chapter 5, I look to the role and impact that transnational advocacy networks have on the Spanish memory movement and the work of the ARMH on the ground. It focuses on the exceptional nature of the exhumations in Guadalajara, Spain, which were a product of the Argentinean-led universal jurisdiction case investigating Franco-era crimes against humanity. The chapter accordingly illustrates the intersecting mechanisms at work during the exhumations that then allow transnational influences to be incorporated into already existing ARMH movement tactics. Additionally, it explores the distinctive consequences created by these transnational relationships between the ARMH and the international community.

5

TRANSNATIONAL NETWORKS

Ascensión Mendieta Ibarra was thirteen years old when she opened the door to the Francoist forces that took her father, Timoteo Mendieta Alcalá—president of a local union. The newly formed Franco regime put Timoteo (among thousands of others) on trial, condemned him to death, and subsequently executed him on November 16, 1939. He was buried in a mass grave with twenty-three other men. He left behind a wife and seven children.

Seventy-four years later, the Argentinean investigative judge Maria Servini de Cubría took testimony from eighty-seven-year-old Ascensión about her family's experience. Armed with Ascensión's testimony, along with over 150 other families, the judge began a long process of demanding accountability for the Franco regime's crimes against humanity, including enforced disappearance, arbitrary detention, torture, and the stealing of babies. For the first time ever, victims of the Spanish Civil War and the Franco regime had finally found a court of law that was willing to listen and demand justice.

This chapter thus simultaneously explores two key ideas. The first is the ARMH's transnational relationships with the international human rights community and how these connections have affected its work and goals. Specifically, I analyze the unique nature of the exhumation of Timoteo Mendieta Alcalá, the intersecting mechanisms at work, which allow the incorporation of transnational actors into ARMH movement tactics, and the distinctive consequences created by these relationships that shape the outcomes of transnational interventions on the ground. My analysis of how global human rights initiatives and actions actually impact the ground efforts in local cases addresses a much-needed, and often undertheorized perspective. The second point suggests how these exhumations, alongside their outcomes (public discussions about the past, funerals, and widespread media coverage), actualize new models of posttransitional justice with global implications.

LEGAL BATTLES, UNIVERSAL JURISDICTION, AND THE TWO EXHUMATIONS OF TIMOTEO

The role and importance of Argentina adjudicating the crimes of Franco reflects the significance of what scholars call transnational advocacy networks (TANs), which are informal groups of actors linked across countries and bound together by shared values, common discourse, and exchanges of service and information (Khagram, Riker, and Sikkink 2002; Tarrow 2001, 2005). Previous scholarship has shown that one of the primary goals of transnational collective action is to create, implement, monitor, and strengthen international laws and norms (Khagram et al. 2002: 4). As such, TANs constitute an emerging and powerful force that has been transforming global practices, especially in human rights (Keck and Sikkink 2014; Risse-Kappen et al. 1999).

Argentina has a long history of human rights TANs that has led to the spread of expertise and tactics, engagement in advocacy, and direct action toward fighting for the rights of victims and helping them gain access to human rights forensics, as was discussed in the first chapter (Zimmerman, Arditti, Brennan and Cavrak 1980; Bouvard 2002; Michel and Sikkink 2013; Sikkink and Walling 2007; Waylen 1994). The case of Timoteo Mendieta, however, highlights the central role that Argentina—and the international community more generally—has played in the recent political struggles over Spain's painful past.

A key aspect of understanding how TANs connect Spain and Argentina is the legal concept of universal jurisdiction, the legal justification for Ascensión giving her testimony in Argentina. Under the international law of universal jurisdiction, any state can claim the authority to prosecute and adjudicate "'core international crimes,' such as crimes against humanity, war crimes, genocide," without having any personal, national, or territorial interest or connection to the crime in question (Langer 2011: 1). In contrast to international criminal tribunals and courts held in one site, universal jurisdiction is decentralized. Universal jurisdiction is consequently a form of legal pluralism, or the idea of having two or more laws or legal systems that coexist within a population or social setting. This dual legal system helps to challenge the sovereignty of individual nation-states in cases where the state is not interested in persecuting certain crimes, such as crimes related to the Civil War or the Franco regime (Michaels 2009). Scholars like Stephanie Golob have connected universal jurisdiction to Habermas's view that the law is like a link or bridge "as the main artery of citizenship and of civil society's influence on the shaping of a 'common good' via government deliberation and administration" (Golob 2008: 135). As such, we can understand the work of forensics-based human rights movements, like the ARMH, as engaging Habermassian principles in three ways: 1) their work functions as consciousness raising via the public forums of their technical work, 2) the use of different legal regimes and pluralisms pushes a "common good" governance even when the state is uninterested, and 3) science functions as the arm of objective truth in the pursuit of long-denied justice. This chapter thus further explores the role of universal jurisdiction in reasserting the illegality of Franco's legacy while simultaneously reaffirming international legal precedents, including the concept that crimes against humanity do not have an expiration date and that justice can be achieved in a variety of ways outside a judicial framework.

The use of universal jurisdiction also fits within the changing legal regimes of transitional justice attempts. As previously mentioned, Spain was originally seen as a transition success story, one to be emulated. As time progressed, transitional politics oscillated from truth commissions to criminal prosecutions, with criminal proceedings becoming more and more emphasized by global courts (see the International Criminal Tribunal for Rwanda, the former Yugoslavia, and the establishment of the permanent International Criminal Court) (Rubin 2014, 2015). Democratic transition preferences have now solidified around the ideals of truth, reparation, and justice (Mihr 2017; Nauenberg 2015; Sikkink 2011).[1]

The International Fight for Justice and the Argentine Complaint (*La Querella Argentina*)

Spanish activists began their international court advocacy in Spanish and European courts (for an expansive view of the process from start to finish, please see fig. 5.1).

Activists, initially inspired by the 2007 historical memory law, filed criminal charges so that Spanish courts would investigate the crimes of the war and the regime. This was possible because,

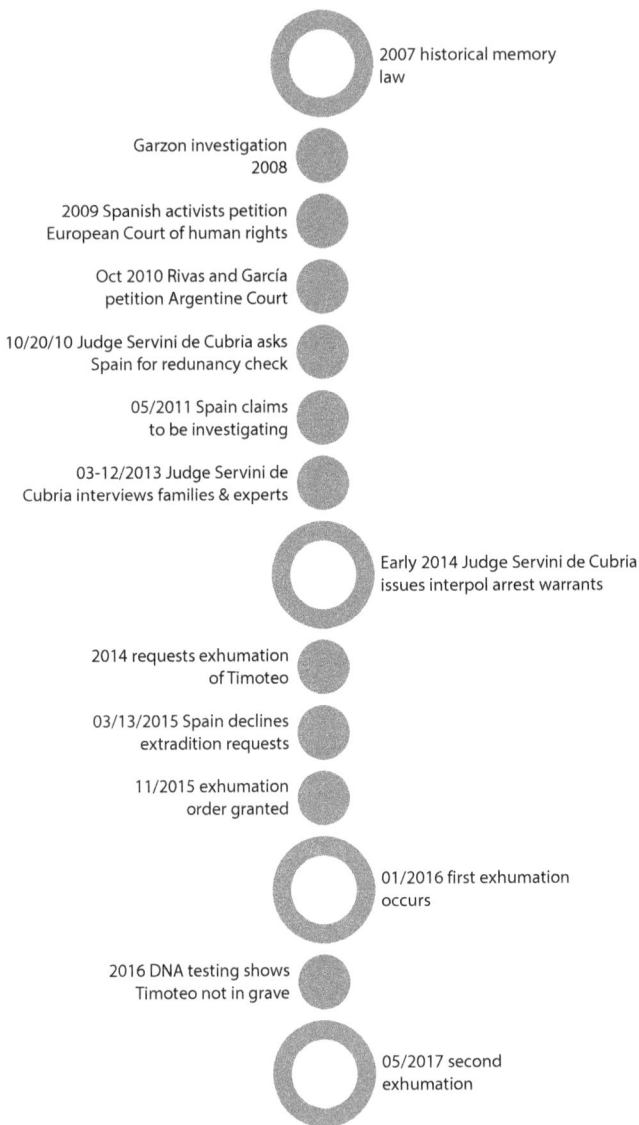

2007 historical memory law

Garzon investigation 2008

2009 Spanish activists petition European Court of human rights

Oct 2010 Rivas and García petition Argentine Court

10/20/10 Judge Servini de Cubria asks Spain for redunancy check

05/2011 Spain claims to be investigating

03-12/2013 Judge Servini de Cubria interviews families & experts

Early 2014 Judge Servini de Cubria issues interpol arrest warrants

2014 requests exhumation of Timoteo

03/13/2015 Spain declines extradition requests

11/2015 exhumation order granted

01/2016 first exhumation occurs

2016 DNA testing shows Timoteo not in grave

05/2017 second exhumation

FIGURE 5.1 Timeline of Spanish Activism and the Argentine Universal Jurisdiction Case against Franco-Era Crimes

unlike in the United States, Spanish citizens have the constitutional right to begin criminal legal proceedings via a "private" prosecution, allowing individual citizens or their representatives to initiate criminal court proceedings. Additionally, judges are also able to investigate crimes.

Judge Baltasar Garzón was the first judge in Spain to take up the cause of Franco-era victims (Burbidge 2011; Hepworth 2020). After a preliminary inquiry in November 2008, Garzón reported his main findings—that during the Civil War and the Franco regime, there had been a clear plan of systematic extermination of civilians and political opponents, which amounted to crimes against humanity (Burbidge 2011; Zapico Barbeito 2010). The decision named high-ranking officials, including General Franco, as responsible. Garzón also ordered that lower courts continue to search for the missing and investigate other low-ranking officials and perpetrators of the violence (Burbidge 2011).

However, on December 2, 2008, the Spanish Supreme Court overturned these decisions, claiming Garzón lacked jurisdiction because, the suspects being dead, they could no longer be criminally liable. The Supreme Court also fully dismissed the case due to the amnesty law of 1977 and statutory limitations (Anon 2008: 67–68). Further, it ordered the lower courts not to investigate cases of enforced disappearances and arbitrary executions that occurred during the war beyond basic record-keeping. Since 2012, hundreds of criminal suits have been dismissed due to the 1977 amnesty law (Anon 2008: 68). Not long after his examination into Franco-era crimes, the Spanish state investigated Garzón for corruption and illegal wiretapping. The Supreme Court cleared him of the corruption charges but found him guilty of illegally wiretapping suspects and subsequently stripped him of his judgeship (Rubin 2016). Many have argued that this was a retaliatory punishment for attempting to upset the status quo about the Francoist past (Ferrándiz 2020; Moreno Fonseret and Candela Sevila 2018).

Nevertheless, Spanish human rights activists persisted and in early 2009 appealed to the European Court of Human Rights, located in Strasbourg, France, to seek redress. In March 2012, the court declared the case inadmissible and would not investigate because the plaintiffs did not bring it to the court in 1979 after the regime transitioned and therefore the statute of limitations had lapsed (Ferrándiz 2020; Moreno Fonseret and Candela Sevila 2018). The court did not consider that in 1979 these families were still too terrified to come forward nor was it common knowledge or practice to use this court.

While Spanish activists faced setbacks addressing these crimes in Europe, Spanish political refugees in Argentina had greater success. In October 2010, Darío Rivas and Inés García Holgado, exiled in Argentina after their parents' murders during the Civil War, brought their case to the Argentinean courts. Both of these activists had become Argentinean citizens during their exile. They were able to bring their case because Argentinean citizens, much like in Spain, have the right to initiate criminal legal investigations, and Argentina had fully embraced the legal concept of universal jurisdiction, due to the state's constitution, ratification of many international treaties, and recent experience with state terror (Langer and Eason 2019; Ugarte 2017). In their complaint they demanded the investigation of cases of crimes against humanity, genocide, enforced disappearance, and the kidnapping of children of political opponents during the war and the regime (Druliolle 2020; Ryan 2017: 70).

On October 14, 2010, the Argentinean investigative judge Maria Servini de Cubría asked Spanish authorities whether courts there were investigating the same case. Initially, the Argentinean court threw out the case because the prosecutor's office in Spain claimed in May 2011 that it was investigating the same crimes. However, further investigation revealed that Spanish authorities had misrepresented the situation, which in turn, pressured the Argentinean court to revisit the case. Judge Servini de Cubría then began taking testimony from victims. By March 2013, over 150 families approached the judge with testimonies. Some of the families also requested that the judge extradite members of the regime for crimes against humanity (Druliolle 2020; Ryan 2017: 299; Ugarte 2017).

The Spanish government, in response to her actions, protested that the case was jeopardizing relations between Argentina and Spain and threatened to issue a formal complaint with the Argentinean embassy (Ryan 2017: 299). Consequently, in March 2013, victims were no longer permitted entry to the Argentinean consulate in Madrid to record testimonies. Servini de Cubría, in response, ordered Argentinean consulates worldwide to record Franco victims' testimonies, thus expanding the reach of the case. She also publicly chided the Spanish state for their obstructionist behavior. In early December 2013, she began cross-examining witnesses and experts in Argentina. She then put out an Interpol extradition request for four former Spanish officials, which Spain denied; two of the men were already dead. In 2014, she issued another extradition request for human rights violations against an additional twenty former Spanish officials, including two government ministers of the Franco regime. On March 13, 2015, Spain declined to extradite these officials, again citing the expiration of the statute of limitations, as these crimes allegedly happened in the 1970s and were past the state's ability to prosecute (Ryan 2017: 299).

In addition, Servini de Cubría officially requested—in 2014—the exhumation of Ascensión's father, Timoteo Mendieta Alcalá, who was believed to be buried in a mass grave in the civil cemetery in Guadalajara, Spain. After some legal wrangling with the Spanish judiciary, the exhumation permission order was granted in late 2015. Despite the detailed request provided, the Spanish judiciary initially denied the request stating that it was uncertain where the body was located. However, a second request restating the precise archival work convinced the Spanish judiciary to approve the exhumation. Thus, for the first time in Spanish history, Spain was compelled by a foreign judge to exhume a victim of the Franco regime. The first exhumation of Timoteo Mendieta Alcalá occurred in January 2016 (Badcock 2016).

However, after the exhumation, extensive DNA testing conducted by the EAAF (Argentine Forensic Anthropology Team) determined that he was not actually in the grave. It was considered that perhaps Timoteo was not biologically related to his children, so his alleged body of was tested against other relatives, known biological cousins. These tests also proved negative. ARMH technicians, after reviewing the cemetery logs, found that another plot and four other individual graves contained the bodies of men who were executed the same day as him. Lawyers working on behalf of the ARMH and the Querella Argentina used this evidence to appeal for a second exhumation order, which they received from Servini de Cubría and the Spanish judiciary in late 2016. The ARMH conducted the second exhumation in May 2017.

It is intriguing why Spain finally decided to capitulate to Argentina when it had blocked previous internal and external pressures to address its history of violence. In some ways, the decision was completely understandable. Argentina, since its transition to democracy in 1983, has led the world in pushing forward human rights regimes and movements. As this book has argued, along with many others, Argentina is the birthplace of forensics-based human rights, a universalist science movement that has radically shifted how human rights interventions take place and created new forms of justice. This includes the conception and diffusion of international human rights laws and treaties that some scholars argue have changed the world's legal regimes to being more human rights conscious and willing to participate in human rights norms (see Sikkink 2011). This history has established Argentina as being a moral authority and state power open and willing to face violent pasts, even when the violations are not explicitly or territorially theirs.

Moreover, the establishment of science-based procedures gives concretized power to those who wield it, whether it is in a global tribunal like the International Criminal Tribunal for the former Yugoslavia or the global forensics-based human rights teams working around the world. As forensics-based human rights has established moral authority alongside scientific legitimacy, it is much harder for nation-states, especially those who claim to be Western democracies, to ignore the call to address their violent pasts and accounts of state terror. Perhaps Argentina, as the originator of forensics-based human rights and a main diffuser of human rights norms and regimes, was the perfect counter to the Spanish state's continued dedication to the status quo.[2] In what follows, I begin the case-study analysis with a brief description of the graveyard.

THE GRAVEYARD OF TIMOTEO: MASS GRAVES AND FRANCOIST MONUMENTS

As described in previous chapters, the ARMH uses different tactics to fight for its movement's goals to combat silence and fear and to present its reframed narrative of the past, all of which support new models of posttransitional justice. The need for

FIGURE 5.2 Franco-era monument to Francoist dead

these types of interventions is apparent as soon as one enters the Guadalajara cemetery. At the entry gate is a commanding monument to those who died for the Francoist cause. The monument is a large grey marble installation with an imposing crucifix and a sign that says, "You Have God and You Guard Spain." Underneath the cross is another sign: "Present!" The local government uses taxes to maintain the monument (see fig. 5.2).

Beyond this monument are two areas that contain mass graves. The larger mass grave containing the remains of more than eight hundred people was destroyed in the 1980s to expand the Catholic cemetery. The bodies were removed, comingled, and buried in an ossuary. Due to these actions, it will never be possible to identify their remains. In this area, local memory activists placed a small strip of grass and installed plaques to mark the Republican dead: "Died for Liberty and Democracy" and "Father We Will Never Forget You."

The second mass grave is closer to the original boundaries of the Catholic cemetery and runs alongside the wall of the larger cemetery. During the late 1930s and early 1940s, this area was the civil part of the cemetery, which held the remains of suicides and unbaptized babies. In my interviews, locals said it had also been a rubbish dump. Once inside the old civil cemetery there is a small plaza-like area with a large fountain and a small statue in the middle of the courtyard.

Along the back wall of the cemetery there are at least sixteen individual plots; some have names affixed to them, and others are in disrepair (see fig. 5.3). The plots are numbered and

FIGURE 5.3 Mass grave plots along the wall of the old civil cemetery

correspond with the official ledgers of the cemetery and contain
the biographical information of those buried in them. However,
as shown in the case with Timoteo, where the ledgers said he
was in plot two but was not, these ledgers are not always accurate. The families of the deceased pay for all upkeep for these
graves, which is a stark contrast to the monument and mausoleum for the Francoist dead. As such, some of the mass grave
plots have no upkeep whatsoever.

An estimated additional 380 people are buried in these graves,
the numbers of the victims roughly corresponding to the cemetery log and military files. Around the middle of the wall are
visible pockmarks from bullet holes, some still holding the metal
fragments of bullets (see fig. 5.4). Due to these marks and bullet
casings discovered at the base of the wall, it is assumed that some

FIGURE 5.4 Bullet holes in the walls in Guadalajara Cemetery

of the victims were executed directly in front of their graves and then thrown in. Oral testimonies from witnesses have also suggested that at least some of the prisoners dug their own graves. One could argue that the state, by leaving such clear marks of mass deaths, was sending a message to the living: Stay silent or face a similar end. With all this in mind, the following analysis unpacks the ARMH's transnational relationships with the international human rights community, how these connections affect and become incorporated into the association's work, and how the outcomes of these transnational interventions (public discussions about the past, funerals, and widespread media coverage), create new models of achievable posttransitional justice.

TECHNICAL WORK AS A PUBLIC FORUM

In the first exhumation in Guadalajara, ARMH workers encountered the common issues of fear and silence when they first attempted to involve the families of the other victims in the grave (located in the second plot of the sixteen individual plots lining the backwall of the cemetery). The ARMH worked with a local memory association to contact the living relatives of the other victims and invite them to the exhumation. This initially proved difficult. One family was vehemently opposed to any sort of exhumation. Yet, as the exhumation was mandated by a judge, their objections were overruled. After begrudgingly witnessing the first exhumation, the family members began to change their minds and, eventually, became avid supporters of the cause and vocal for the rights of the families of the victims. In fact, one of the grandchildren became very active and has been trying to find a way to get the criminal convictions of her grandfather and the other executed prisoners removed from their records. The second exhumation led to the identification of this woman's grandfather, who was reburied in 2018. Neither this identification and reburial, nor the granddaughter's activist involvement, would have been possible had it not been for the Argentinean universal jurisdiction case.

However, in spite of the foreboding nature of the cemetery and the initial reluctance from some of the victims' families, the 2017 exhumation was entirely different in regards to fear. In all of my informal interviews with visitors, I was surprised to find a lack of trepidation while discussing the past or criticizing the state. This might have been because many of these visitors were city dwellers, not villagers who had directly experienced repression. Many of these visitors might not have had victims in their family lines. The lack of fear might also have reflected the groundwork created by the first exhumation in 2016 and a selection effect of who was visiting the second exhumation. During the first exhumation, the victims' families received an outpouring of national and international support, including a deluge of positive domestic and international media coverage, visitors, and supportive messages sent to the ARMH.

Whatever created the welcoming atmosphere, the willingness to talk candidly about the past was further encouraged by the public space created by the technical fieldwork site. Much like the ARMH's other forensic interventions, visitors used the exhumation site to engage in both political speech and criticism of the controlling powers of Spain. This exhumation was unique in how often visitors organically started to critique the state while socializing near the gravesite. Criticizing the state, of course, is not explicitly connected to transnational advocacy or networks. However, in this case, the exhumation in its very essence is a reflection of the influence of international interventions—as a foreign state was involved from the start. As such, the international nature of the exhumation may have allowed for a clearer sense of the Spanish state's failings for the average visitor at the exhumation.

Most of the people I interviewed criticized the current government, pointing to their lack of support for the exhumations as proof of political malfeasance. As one woman in her fifties, Ana Maria, said, "This government is not a democracy; it is a continuance of the dictatorship." Her husband, Francisco, agreed: "If the transition had returned to the original Second Republic constitution instead of creating a new one, then things would have been very different and better." This is an interesting thought, as the new constitution is less progressive in some ways than the original.

Intriguingly, almost all of my informal interviewees stated that the government was not actually democratic, just a continuation of the regime. To make this point, many used the current political structure and leaders to illustrate how little has changed in Spain since the time of Franco. For example, one woman, Laura, who arrived with her husband and two sons, explained, "This is not really a democracy, and to have a prime minister like Rajoy saying that the government will never give money to support these efforts is evidence of that. This is not a finished story in Spain. If we were over it, then there would not be a problem of supporting and doing exhumations. But it is still a problem, because we are not dealing with our past." For many, Prime Minister Rajoy and the former ruling government are emblematic of the larger tradition of ignoring the past while simultaneously denigrating the victims.

Similarly, others connected the maintenance of Francoism to those in the ruling right-wing People's Party (PP). As one older woman, Dolores, who lost family members to Francoist violence and whose grandmother suffered incarceration and gendered violence, said, "The families, we remember, we guard everything within ourselves. It is they [the PP] who want to erase everything. But we remember everything. They keep trying to say that we are the bad ones and that all we want is money, like the spokesperson for PP. They are without shame. We are the good ones here and they are just shameless." Another man argued that the "PP is worse than the fascists; because they pretend that they are not." Many also mentioned the hypocrisy of the right-wing Aznar government in the early 2000s, who paid to exhume and repatriate the bodies of nationals who fought in the Blue Division alongside Hitler on the Eastern Front. Yet, as already noted, Rajoy publicly announced that the government would never give money to exhume the victims of the Spanish Civil War and Francoist repression. The fact that the Spanish government was willing to use taxpayer money to repatriate bodies buried on foreign soil while fighting for Hitler but had to be compelled by a foreign judge to exhume some of the victims of the regime made the hypocrisy of the government particularly notable for the visitors.

Another man in his fifties, Patricio, whose great-uncle lies in a mass grave somewhere in Zaragoza, argued, "In Spain, it is always one step forward and two steps back. Take the socialists; they tried to change things with their historical memory law, but it was flawed because it made memory privatized; it put all the responsibility on the individual and not on the government for taking responsibility for the actions of the past." According to this view, the bad memory politics of Spain were not just associated with the conservative government but rather the larger state. Regardless of who is currently in power, the government has always been unwilling to take responsibility for its past, which is exactly how Spanish activists ended up relying on international courts to help them force the issue.

Nevertheless, some informants said their ability to speak their mind about the government and to have scientific exhumations of the missing are signs that things have changed dramatically since the democratic transition and even within the last twenty years. These interlocutors still maintained that human rights advocates still had much work left to do to change the culture and the political structure. Despite the critical view of the current government and whether it is actually democratic, many also expressed hope that this particular exhumation, due to its connection to the Argentinean universal jurisdiction trial, would help to wake up their fellow Spaniards to face the past. As one visitor, Anita, explained, "Exhumations bring change, even if it is slow. It is important that the people see these things, to see the violence, because it is here, completely naked for everyone to see." Angela, a Madrid local in her fifties, voiced similar sentiments while watching the removal of the first body: "See that! One has been recovered so far, and that is one less in the ground. That is a victory." Across all interviews, respondents agreed that exhumations, and in particular the exhumations at Guadalajara due to their transnational nature, were important to the country. They were important because they brought international attention to the "truth" of the past and the continued plight of the families of the missing.

Surprisingly, everyone I spoke to in Guadalajara said that exhumations were important for the future of Spain. This viewpoint was a stark difference from previous exhumations in local villages, where many expressed their concern that these interventions would bring more violence and destabilize the government or that, these wounds should stay closed. In fact, visitors in Guadalajara consistently mocked the idea that past wounds would ever close. Hector, a man in his thirties, expressed, "It is insane for anyone to say that the past is in the past, or that we shouldn't be opening old wounds, because they were never closed to begin with. If they were, then this wouldn't be such a big story." He continued: "Things are changing, and these exhumations are pushing people to talk and push for change more than ever before." Informants often credited exhumations as being the medium for change because, they argued, they showed the "truth" of the past. This seemed to reinforce the ARMH's framing and argument for both the need for forensic science and their version of the past. Yet, the heterogeneity of political belief, again, may be reflective of a selection effect. The vast majority of visitors had made the decision to visit; they didn't just stumble upon an exhumation on the way to the market.

That said, not all visitors to the graveyard had come for the exhumation. In Spain, especially for older generations, the culture still supports the idea that graveyards and plots should be well maintained. To do otherwise is shameful. Thus, townspeople were constantly wandering by to check on their loved ones' graves, which provided continual interaction with people to whom I could talk about the past and their opinions on the work of the association. In one of my interviews with Cristina, a local woman in her late seventies who tended her husband's grave almost daily, she mentioned she had also witnessed the exhumation the year before. She did not want to see the exhumation itself, for fear of seeing bodies, but said that even though it had all happened so long ago, she really hoped that Ascensión would be able to find her father. She said she was glad that Ascensión had found a way to make it happen, even if it meant having to go to Argentina. "Can you imagine? To go all that way to be able to find your father? What a fighter." For Cristina, the simplicity and humanity of Ascensión's fight to get her father back is what made the exhumation compelling.

Others I spoke with felt that the case of Guadalajara, unlike other exhumations, was also able to shine a very bright light on the Spanish state's dedication to repressing the "defeated," even forty years after the democratic transition. Many informants gave the example of the ongoing battles with the city government over what to do with the identified remains from the first exhumation.

In 2016, all the exhumed bodies underwent DNA testing in an attempt to return them to their families. One of the bodies identified was that of a man whose son regularly attended the first exhumation. On the day the team was digging up the purported body of his father, the man showed up with a burlap bag.[3] The lead archeologist asked him why he had the bag, and the son responded, "So I can finally take my father home with me." The team eventually convinced him to wait for the DNA testing to come through.

After DNA had identified all the bodies from the 2016 exhumation, the team expected to give the bodies back to the families. However, the local government of Guadalajara did not want the identified remains removed from the Madrid lab where they were being stored—the judge's order was *only* for the exhumation of Timoteo Mendieta Alcalá. Essentially, officials wanted the ARMH to create a modern mass grave and continue to prohibit the relatives from burying their dead. After a lot of bad press and pressure from civil society groups, the local government eventually backed down and agreed to allow the remaining families to take custody of their loved ones' remains and artifacts. It should be noted that the larger centralized state did nothing in support of the families' rights to get their loved ones back. The EAAF identified the father of the man with the burlap bag, and on May 19, 2018, he was returned to his family in an homage ceremony conducted by the ARMH.

This reluctance to return the identified remains of repression victims illuminates the government's commitment to maintaining the stratified system set up by the Franco regime, which prioritized the winners—the Francoists—and ensured the defeated—the

Republicans—were forever labeled as scorned traitors to the nation. Additionally, the local government's behavior also shows the damage of maintaining a sanitized silence about the past. The pact of forgetting was argued as necessary to keep the peace, but in this case, among countless others, silencing was used to preserve the power structure of the Franco regime, effectively keeping the Francoist state in power over both the body politic and the historical narrative of the past, the outcome of which is the continued stigmatization of the defeated and glorification of the Francoist cause. Thus, *any* exhumations and eventual reburial of the Republican dead is a significant victory (and a form of justice) over the centralized state's continued and determined refusal to reincorporate the "enemy dead" back into the citizenry. Visitors thus rightly see the work of the memory movement and actions like exhumations as a form of long-awaited justice for the families and as a triumph over how Spain should remember and acknowledge its past.

Thoughts about Argentina's Intervention in Spanish Politics

Not surprisingly, the visitors had a great deal to say about Argentina being the catalyst for the exhumation. People expressed a wide range of emotions when discussing a foreign judge's role in the exhumation, let alone a judge from a former colony. Lucia, a woman in her thirties, said she was "very angry" that this case was brought by an Argentinean judge and did not happen via the Spanish system. She said, "This is a reflection of how taboo the past still is. People are still afraid to talk." Lucas, a Madrid local in his forties, agreed: "The fact that this had to be ordered by Argentina is a reflection of just how bad things are here in Spain."

Another woman in her sixties, Carla, who has been unable to exhume her relative from another plot in the cemetery, agreed, arguing that the historical memory law was worthless in actually helping families. She continued, "The only reason this exhumation is happening is because of the judge in Argentina. Think about that. If it was up to our local government, they would have stayed there forever." Many others similarly felt that if it had not been for the actions of Servini de Cubría, the bodies from those two plots would still be buried as their murderers had intended, lost in oblivion.

Others were more pointed in their opinion of the Argentinean intervention. Enrique, a volunteer in his mid-thirties, came almost every day to help with the work. He was motivated by the fact that he had a great-grandfather and a great-uncle buried there. During a formal interview, he was more critical of the state: "To me Argentina's involvement is shameful, because it is a reflection of how our government has dealt with the past. Whether it be the Amnesty Law, the Law of Historical Memory, these were actually only just used as political weapons. They were not used for the purpose they should have been, which in this case, would be acting in accordance with international human rights. They have simply been used as a political weapon to throw in the face of victims and gain more votes." For Enrique, Argentina stepping in was a reflection of the Spanish state's continued failure to use its own political structure to end the marginalization of the defeated. Consequently, Argentina's intervention was shameful, not only because Spaniards had to rely on another country to help but also because Spain's own government had been unable to evolve past Franco-era thinking.

However, others attempted to contextualize the role of Argentina within the political landscape of Spain and changing international human rights standards. During a formal interview with

Ricardo, a family member to a victim buried there, and regular volunteer at the exhumation, he gave me his opinion:

> Fortunately, this kind of thing [universal jurisdiction] exists. . . . If it did not exist, then what would you do? If this had not happened before, with Garzón and the attempted prosecution of Pinochet then we would have ended up in the same vicious cycle. Spain is an example of prolonged repression, which has been agreed to between the repressors, so as to reach a transition agreement. In many cases, the law of silence ends up just reinforcing the same repression. If there are no external agents that are able to act, there is no way out of this vicious cycle. And impunity, if not stopped, encourages repetition.

For Ricardo, the fight against impunity is a global one. As he also pointed out, Garzón began the global responsibility of universal jurisdiction in his attempt to hold the ex-dictator of Chile, Augusto Pinochet, accountable. Argentina has now picked up where the Spaniards left off. Ricardo clearly articulated how important transnational connections and the upholding of international human rights can be, especially when nation-states like Spain do not want to hold themselves accountable for past atrocities.

Similarly, in my conversations with other visiting relatives of the victims, the role of Argentina was seen as a practical choice. Lydia, a relative of one of the victims in one of the other plots said, "The Argentine intervention is good because it has made things happen. We have to use all our available resources. It is an injustice that we cannot get our loved ones back, they are ours." This quote highlights that human rights workers and family members alike consider transnational advocacy networks an integral aspect of achieving transitional justice.

Across the informants, there was a mix of anger and gratitude about Argentina's role in Spain's ongoing battle over its
violent past. For those without a direct connection to the violence, it seemed astonishing that activists had to go to South
America to get some semblance of justice. Argentina's intervention illuminated the Spanish state's actual interests in maintaining the status quo of sanitized silence and its perpetual oblivion
and repression of Franco victims. For the families of the victims,
Spain's inaction was not surprising but still deeply disappoint-
ing. They were grateful, however, that they could force Spain
to comply even if it meant relying on a foreign government.
Indeed, Argentina's intervention in Spanish memory politics
is an extraordinary development in human rights regimes
and is illustrative of the rising power of international law and
TANs. Furthermore, these exhumations are the actualization of
new and clearly achievable posttransitional justice for long-ago
state terror.

THE NEW INTERNATIONAL BRIGADES

In both of the Guadalajara exhumations, foreign forensic
anthropologists worked concurrently with the exhumation process to help speed up the anthropological analysis of the remains.
The involvement of foreign forensic experts also helped bring
more attention to the case while ensuring that the work conducted would be admissible in the Argentinean courts. At the
second exhumation, a team of forensic experts from the United
Kingdom flew in to help with the immediate anthropological
analysis. Because of Ascensión's advanced age (ninety-one at the
second exhumation), the analysis of the remains and DNA sampling of the bones was done concurrently with the exhumation

to increase the odds of her surviving to witness the results. Consequently, the DNA analysis was done at a much faster rate than after the first exhumation.

International Forensic Experts and Pedagogy

The role of the foreign experts, however, was not solely technical. As at other observed exhumations, the ARMH incorporated the foreign experts into their "pedagogical" approach of teaching people about the science of the work and the goals of the association.

Although there were constant visitors, ARMH leaders did not run large classes for attendees as they did with most other observed exhumations. They instead would engage with visitors using variations of their technical classes. The reason for this was simple: they had more to show, which allowed the ARMH to teach in parts.

All classes started with an explanation of how these killings were the result of postwar repression and that in this case the Francoists had thoroughly documented their violence. ARMH technicians would pass around a copy of the cemetery record book to show visitors how cemetery workers had counted and cataloged the victims. The classes sometimes also included a tour of the cemetery. A volunteer ballistics aficionado would explain the various Mauser bullets he found in the ground and discuss the various bullet holes and fragments stuck in the cemetery wall, often displaying the bullets on top of a headstone or out on the table (see fig. 5.5).

Many visitors were taken to the location—originally an autopsy room at the cemetery—where the British forensic team was working. The lead forensic expert worked in the main entry hall, reconstructing skulls, while the other three worked on

FIGURE 5.5 ARMH volunteer shows bullet casings to visitors

cleaning and articulating the remains while also cataloging any perimortem or postmortem injuries, as well as making judgments on the sex of the remains and age at the time of death.

Two of the four experts, who were bilingual, did the talking during visits. They would go into detail explaining how forensic anthropology tells the stories of the bones, or what happened during the lives of the victims. For example, for one group, the lead forensic anthropologist explained how a male victim in his mid-twenties had been shot at point-blank range in the back of the head and how the bullet traveled through his cranium—the trajectory of the bullet demonstrated with a red stir stick. The anthropologist then commented on how he knew that, as a child, the man had at least one high fever because of the rings that showed up on his teeth. The other anthropologists explained how they could determine sex and age by pointing out markers (pelvic width and cranial notches) on remains they were working on. Although the ARMH's lead archeologist normally did this kind of technical explanation, in this case he handed off this task to the foreign professionals.

In this way, the ARMH seamlessly transferred the responsibilities for teaching the validity and importance of the technical work to the international volunteers. This aspect of the ARMH's pedagogical tactic justified its depoliticized stance and the results of its technical work, not to mention the veracity of its reframed narrative of the violence. By integrating the British forensic experts into teaching visitors how to understand the stories that the bones are telling, the ARMH was also bolstering the legitimacy of the ARMH's version of Spain's recent violent past.

During one class, the forensics experts reenacted how they believed one of the victims was executed. Placing one of the older male experts on his knees, the female expert moved her fingers to a cocked position (to simulate a gun) at the back of his head and demonstrated the exact angle and proximity they believed the executioner used on his victim. The experts then showed the actual injuries on the skeletal remains to further demonstrate their findings. In another instance, they presented the scapula of a man who had been previously shot in the back, possibly during the Civil War, and whose wound had been healing at the time of his execution. One of the experts said, "That's some terrible luck."

The forensic experts also told those listening that they had been finding a lot of evidence of torture and pointed out that many of the men's ribs were broken on both sides, suggesting severe beatings. Others had broken or shattered arm and leg bones that had just started to heal, meaning that they had occurred while the men had been imprisoned. This information was new for many, as torture, for some unknown reason, had never really been associated with these detentions. Most thought the men had just been detained and then summarily executed, rather than having been terribly brutalized before being killed. The news about the victims having first been tortured was also surprising to many of the ARMH. Echoing Dr. Clyde Snow in Argentina, the forensic experts said, "The bones don't lie."

Several people said they found the forensic experts' explanations more upsetting than seeing the bodies in the actual grave. One visitor, Gabriel, a twenty-year-old student in Madrid, said, "Having someone show you, this is the pathology of a person, this is what their bones tell us about what they suffered through at the time of their internment and then say, 'this is where the entry wound was, and this is the position they were executed in,' just definitely humanized the bones into becoming a person." Therefore, the international forensic volunteers brought a level of expertise and impartiality that was important for many of the visitors to see the true brutality of the Franco regime. For others, the participation of foreigners, including myself, signified two things: 1) the beginning of the new international brigades, or a new version of international volunteers trying to help fight for democracy in Spain; and 2) the shamefulness that Spaniards will not do this for themselves. As one technically trained volunteer, Pascal, said, "No offense, but this should be Spaniards who are here. It should be Spaniards who are doing all of this. I find it so very sad and pathetic that we have to rely on foreigners to get this done."

TRANSNATIONAL RELATIONSHIPS, INTERNATIONAL COLLECTIVE MEMORY, AND PERFORMANCE

In addition to the influence that Argentina had on the exhumations, another transnational relationship became apparent, and that was with Norway. In the last decade, the ARMH has developed and cultivated a relationship with a Norwegian electrical union, which donates a considerable sum of money every year to the ARMH. The relationship with the Norwegian trade union is important because it speaks to the existence of a European community, not explicitly based in human rights activism but one that is still dedicated to supporting international human rights.[4] This relationship with the Norwegian trade union and the ARMH illustrates an interesting variation of TANs that is working to influence the spread and strengthening of international human rights norms. Additionally, the collaboration also suggests that the ARMH has been successful at challenging the Spanish state's official narrative of the past violence while also spreading and reinforcing its reframed collective memory at an international level.

When asked how the relationship with the ARMH formed, the union leader explained that it had to do with the union's historical relationship with fellow unionists during the Spanish Civil War. During the war, the Norwegians had supported Spanish trade unionists and had even attempted to get them out of Spain. He said the union's contributions to the ARMH were in honor of that bond, "as well as that between those who work in unions, and the democratic ideals that they, as members of the European Economic Area, want to protect and uphold." During the second exhumation in Guadalajara, a delegation from the Norwegian Electrical Union came to visit. Its members were treated to a full-scale class led by the vice president, the ARMH's ballistic aficionado, the lead archeologist, and the British forensic experts. They spent many hours with the team, talked with relatives of the victims, and ate lunch with everyone near the gravesite. During my informal interviews, many of the Norwegians similarly connected their support of the ARMH to their belief in unions and democracy. Lucas, a man in his early thirties, said, "We are here as a union, and we have this philosophy where we are not just thinking of ourselves; we have to help other unions around Europe and in our country. We support the association because we feel that it is important to support our democratic ideals and the rights that we as people have." For many of the Norwegians, their union's monetary support of the ARMH was a reflection of their dedication to their belief in unions and democracy.

The majority of the Norwegians also voiced their dismay that promotion of fascism, including the giant monument to the fascist dead at the entrance of the cemetery, could exist in modern and mainland Europe. As Emil, who was in his forties, said, "This fascist monument is shocking. I think something like this—you do not see something like this in Norway. This would not be acceptable. It would not be acceptable because we believe in equality and fairness among people." Many of the Norwegian visitors referred to Norway's own history with the Nazis and how important it had been for Norwegians to confront their past. One young woman, Sophie, said, "Seeing this kind of inspires me to get more involved in fighting more for our democracy and what our parents and grandparents fought for us to have." Another member, a man in his sixties, Henrik, said that he was glad that he had been able to see the work of the ARMH because his father had fought in the Spanish Civil War in the international brigades as a young man before fighting in the Second World War. Through his tears, he said that he was glad to know that he had been able to help, even if it was in some small way, to continue the fight against fascism as a testament to his father.

Interestingly, the majority of Spanish visitors to the Guadalajara exhumation also consistently compared the state of Spain's memory politics with that of Germany. One couple in

their mid-thirties arrived with their young son, who after seeing the hole in the ground, wanted to know where the dinosaurs
were. The wife was a German national and the couple expressed
how different it was in Germany. The husband, Hugo, said, "In
Germany they don't shy away from the past. We should do that
here, so we do not end up reliving it." Others similarly compared
Germany's memory work, including creating museums, while
also fully addressing the country's past, as something that Spain
should emulate. A common refrain was "The Germans did it
right" or "Look at Germany." Again, this was a major difference
among the other observed exhumations, where no one referred
to Germany as being the ideal model of how to handle its violent
past. This may be reflective of the fact that many of the visitors to
the Guadalajara exhumation lived in Madrid, had traveled outside of Spain, had been exposed to more foreigners also living
in Madrid and, on the whole, were better educated than people
living in more rural areas of Spain.

Like many of their Spanish counterparts who had no familial connection to the violence, the majority of Norwegians
expressed their amazement at what they were witnessing. One
young woman in her twenties, Mia, who works on overhead
power lines, said, "This work is really inspiring. I think it is really
sad that the Spanish government doesn't support it. It is their
job to do this. I think it is really good that Argentina is helping."
Like others, Mia also criticized the Spanish state for failing to
uphold its responsibilities to confront the past and take care of
the victims of its past state terror.

Others pointed out the paradox that Argentina is pushing for
justice. Sander, a middle-aged man, said, "It is ironic that it is
Argentina, because they used to be a violent military regime and
even went to war over the Falkland Islands; they were the bad
guys and now they are good guys!" Thus, for some, the ability to

give money and visit the work of the ARMH was inspirational, as well as a reminder that fascism is not just a problem for the history books.

For many of the Norwegians, it was completely incomprehensible that the Catholic Church had been so involved in the regime. During their class discussion with the lead archeologist, one man asked, "Well, can't the Church intercede on behalf of the families? Surely they can help." This comment was met with complete silence, and the ARMH official photographer jumped in to explain that the Catholic Church had been complicit in the violence. He pointed out that according to local legend a priest had been directly involved in the executions of the Guadalajara prisoners; he had been the person to fire the second shot to the head to ensure that prisoners were in fact dead. That priest is buried in the same cemetery as his victims, albeit in a different part, with an ornate grave marker. The Norwegians were appalled by this story, with one man, Alexander, saying, "It is so surprising to learn this. It is surreal to think that someone who should have mercy would be going around killing people. It is quite ironic." The photographer then took the Norwegians to go see the priest's grave and to see where the larger mass grave had been.

Across almost all of my informal interviews with the Norwegians, they mentioned how important it was for people worldwide to know the "truth" about what happened in Spain. As one man, William, said, "It is very emotional to see this. It is so much more impactful in person. My hope is that something like this will never happen again. It is important to know the history. This is a part of Europe. We have to give this lesson to the next generation." The Norwegians believed the "truth" of the ARMH's narrative of the historical past in large part to what they had seen at the exhumation. With many pointing out that, they did not believe the centralized state's version of the past to be true, with many highlighting that they felt that this history did not only belong to Spain but rather to all of Europe. Due to this collective ownership of history, many have argued, like William, that this history should not be buried but taught as an integral part of preventing another round of fascism in Europe and the world (Albright 2019).

After lunch, the Norwegians went across the street to escape the heat of the day and get a drink. They later reappeared at the gravesite, each holding a red rose. The leader of the union said that they wanted to pay their respects to their fellow union members and human beings before they left. He thanked the ARMH and its volunteers for their tireless work to restore the humanity of the missing. He then asked members of the public to bow their heads in a moment of silence. The visiting Spaniards, including many associated with the ARMH, and journalists seemed stunned at what was happening. The union leader then walked very carefully along the edge of the grave, which at this point was a deep hole, and placed a red rose up against the wall behind it. Again he paused and gave what looked like a silent prayer then walked back to the group. One by one, the rest, about fifteen in total, left roses (see fig. 5.6). After the last rose was laid in place, everyone applauded with some wiping tears from their eyes. One of the journalists covering the exhumation turned to me and said, "Finally, they got a funeral." Later the ARMH leadership announced that the Norwegian Electrical Union had donated over 6,000 Euros to the ARMH so that the association could continue its work.

The Norwegian Electrical Union's relationship with the ARMH is thus another example of the importance of TANs that support the norms and practices, which uphold the importance of human rights. Importantly, this example demonstrates another variation of creating and actualizing new models of posttransitional justice. The Norwegians, during their visit, engaged with

FIGURE 5.6 View from inside the grave with roses above

secular death rituals by holding a mini-funeral. The relationship between the Norwegians and the ARMH also gives further international recognition and approval of the ARMH's narrative of the history of violence in Spain. If the union did not believe the ARMH's narrative, it would not support the association's work. Furthermore, this relationship provides a clear example of how TANs can subvert a nation-state's sovereignty over a historical narrative of past state violence, as well as how these relationships spread and reinforce a reframed collective memory transnationally at a microinterpersonal level.

TRANSNATIONAL MEDIA DIFFUSION

Due to the historic and transnational nature of the Guadalajara exhumations, the ARMH received a lot of news coverage, both international and domestic. Throughout both exhumations, the ARMH leadership conducted countless interviews broadcast through a variety of news media across the world (Badcock 2017; Dowsett 2016; Frayer 2016; Neuman 2017). While the press coverage was inevitable, it would be inaccurate to say that the ARMH did not capitalize on the opportunity presented by the media. Rather, the ARMH strategically used the Guadalajara exhumations to spread and reinforce the importance of their work and goals, while also introducing their reframed narrative of the collective memory of the past violence in Spain. They then reposted all the media coverage to their social media accounts, further diffusing the exposure. After one popular Spanish news program covered the first exhumation, the ARMH's website crashed due to all the online visitors.

Moreover, the exceptional and transnational nature of the Guadalajara exhumations also provided a stage for other human rights organizations and groups to similarly benefit. For example, many documentary filmmakers covering the topic of universal jurisdiction, and others focusing on the historical memory movement came to film both exhumations. During the second exhumation, a documentary film crew from Amnesty International Spain came to film the work. Part of this delegation included members from the Madrid office of Amnesty who also filmed little videos with the lead archeologist to put on their social media (Spain 2017). Amnesty International Spain posted the videos alongside calls for more attention to the exhumation, the importance of the universal jurisdiction case, and the continued suffering of Spaniards at the hands of the state.

Coverage from Amnesty International and the international press demonstrate an additional example as to how TANs use technology, like social media and the Internet, to expand and solidify the ideas and importance of human rights practices. Moreover, the ARMH, Amnesty International, and the universal jurisdiction case benefit from the media coverage, as it spreads the idea of international human rights law, the need for international accountability, and the very belief that global human rights are important even when delayed. The media coverage also gave activists and the technicians a global platform to clearly argue their case, put pressure on the Spanish state, and introduce this topic to people who might not otherwise know about the violence that happened in Spain. As such, international media coverage that diffuses a re-framed narrative of the violence should also be considered an achievable model of justice in cases of long ago violence and where the state is uninterested in pursuing legal justice, as it provides a wider transmission of new historical truths that circumnavigates the intent of the nation-state.

The ARMH has also used Ascensión as the face of the victims to gain sympathy and support for their cause. Ascensión is a little old woman, who speaks clearly and eloquently about the pain and suffering of losing her father to state terror. It would be politically risky to tell her she should not be able to find her father before she dies, which she has said many times on camera, is her final wish. Interestingly, during most interviews that Ascensión conducted during her father's exhumations, she did not mention the politics that led to her father's death. Instead, she focused solely on the desire to find and respectfully bury her father before her own death. That is not to suggest that she is a completely depoliticized activist, as she speaks plainly on her political beliefs and her critiques of the state. She, like the ARMH, just did not do it during the exhumation process, because to do so would associate the exhumation itself with politics, potentially delegitimizing it.

Ascensión is well aware of her role. She is a savvy activist and has done countless media interviews with some of the most popular and well-watched Spanish news shows, where she has used the platform to advance her goals in fighting for the rights of the victims. Many people spoke of Ascensión as a *luchadora* or a fighter, as a hero, and an example for others. She has won numerous human rights awards in Spain, further putting her name and cause in the news. Most recently in April 2018 she and her lawyer, Ana Messuti, won the Historical Memory Award, given to them by the left-wing, United Left Party. The United Party gave them the award because, "They are two women who developed a fundamental role in the Argentinean lawsuit in the defense of historical memory in our country, so that we may have justice, truth, and reparation" (Bachiller 2018). Her case has brought a lot of attention to the few surviving direct descendants of the Republican dead, as well as the long lasting and torturous effect that enforced disappearance and state terror has on families. Her image has also become part of political cartoons and street graffiti in Madrid (see photo).

FIGURE 5.7 Graffiti in Madrid: "Dignity is always a fight. The fight is always dignity."

THE CONTINUED IMPACT OF ARGENTINA'S INTERVENTION AND NEW MODELS OF JUSTICE

Although it may take years to fully know how the Argentinean universal jurisdiction case has affected Spain, we can look at its impact on different levels, the micro and meso Spanish society levels and the macro, global level. At the macro level, this case demonstrates how exhumations and their outcomes (public discussions about the past, pedagogy, memory events, widespread media coverage) actualize new models of posttransitional justice in cases where the state is uninterested or hostile to pursuing justice for past violence. This case also demonstrates that these new forms of justice can be successfully actualized through a combination of both top down and bottom up efforts by both local and transnational human rights forces produced by intersecting actors like activists, lawyers, international judges, trade unionists, and scientists. In the coming years it will be interesting to see if other cases of past violence where victims have been denied access to legal justice or where the violence is from the long ago past will use these models of postjustice. This would seem to be the case, as activists in Indonesia have begun some of these efforts to recover, identify, and rebury victims from the 1965 genocide and the Suharto regime, as well as in Tulsa, Oklahoma, where efforts have been made to find, recover, and identify victims of the 1921 Black Wall Street massacre.

The Argentinean universal jurisdiction case against Spain has also become an example of how the world can participate in demanding justice for victims in other countries. In a broader sense, the Argentinean universal jurisdiction case against Franco-era crimes seems to provide a potential path for other countries similarly facing state obstruction and amnesty policies.

The Argentinean investigation and universal jurisdiction trial has consequently created and reinforced the legal precedent for other cases in states elsewhere to move forward. The 2021 universal jurisdiction court case in Germany used to convict a Syrian military official of crimes against humanity, suggests that other countries can and will use these precedents to maintain the belief of human rights, international law regimes, as well as the idea that no war criminal is safe from prosecution and accountability (Colangelo 2021).

Changes in Spain

At the meso Spanish societal levels there have also been some immediate changes. Due to this case, over 105 people have been exhumed from mass graves with the majority successfully identified. The reburial of these individuals is ongoing. Additionally, in 2020 the ARMH was able to successfully exhume all the bodies from plot 3, with another twenty-four people currently undergoing forensic analysis and identification. This third exhumation was completed without the need for foreign intervention and was not contested by the local government, which was a tremendous indication of the kind of power and influence these types of transnational interventions can have on local memory and justice projects.

The case has also led to changes in how some regional governments in Spain have come to understand the past violence. It should be noted that the regional governments (Basque and Catalan) that were the most inspired by the Argentinean universal jurisdiction case are located in areas that historically suffered the most during the war and under the Franco regime, have clear regional political identities that are often secessionist in nature, and tend to be more critical of the centralized Spanish government. Their mobilization after the universal jurisdiction case may reflect the fact that until the Argentinean case became a reality, these regions lacked the opportunity structure, or access to political institutions, to address the past violence (McAdam 1996). The impact of universal jurisdiction, as an aspect of a new transnational opportunity structure, is illustrative of how transnational interventions and advocacy can empower certain actors to build new political and legal regimes that present a different collective memory of the past that runs counter to the centralized state's version.

In 2013, in the immediate aftermath of Spain's obstruction of Judge Servini de Cubría's investigation, the Basque parliament moved into action, passing a law that gave its support to the Argentinean case (Ryan 2017: 300–301). The law also claimed the 1936 coup was illegal and condemned the regime's repression of the Basque and Catalan cultures and regions. Moreover, the Basque parliament denounced the amnesty law of 1977. On November 29, 2013, representatives of the Basque government went to Buenos Aires and met with Servini de Cubría, as well as the Mothers and Grandmothers of the Plaza de Mayo.

In November 2013, the local parliament of Navarra, which is an autonomous community and province in northern Spain and part of the larger Basque region, backed the Foral Law of Historical Memory (La Ley Foral de la Memoria Histórica), attempting to fix the perceived imperfections of the historical memory law. Under this law, the Navarra regional government assumes the cost of exhumations, not only in its territory but also beyond, if a Navarran citizen requests one. Moreover, the law provides extensive technical, psychological, and economic support to help the families of the missing. It also gives financial support to build a local DNA bank to help with the identification process. A space has also been reserved in the Pamplona cemetery for the unidentified remains of victims, while honors provided to the Francoists have been removed.

Importantly, the law also rescinded all judicial sentences and convictions issued by Francoist courts in the region. The Navarran government ordered schools to revise their history courses to convey a more balanced history of the past. The Foral Law of Historical Memory also pledged to erect a monument in any European death camp where a Navarran citizen perished as a way of combating collective amnesia about Spaniards who were disappeared at the end of the Civil War (Ryan 2017: 300–301).

Before the more recent developments in Catalonia, there had also been a movement to similarly address the past violence.[5] In October 2013, the left-wing Esquerra Republicana de Catalunya approached Servini de Cubría to investigate the murder of the ex-president of the Generalitat, or Catalan parliament, Lluís Companys. The judge initiated an investigation later that same year. In Asturias, another region in the northwest of Spain, the parliament voted to condemn the legacy of Franco and the repression of Republicans. The parliament correspondingly pledged to set up mechanisms for truth and reconciliation in the region. They also encouraged their citizens to continue denouncing abuses to Servini de Cubría in Buenos Aires (Ryan 2017: 300–01).

Additionally, other regional governments—again in areas that historically suffered from Francoist repression—are attempting to either participate in or support the Argentinean universal jurisdiction case. This seems to suggest that at one level, the Argentinean transnational interference has been successful at helping civil society groups and regional and local governments gain a foothold in pushing against the status quo.

While the actual legal consequences for the Spanish state may seem minimal in comparison to other countries that have faced judicial trials, such as the International Criminal Tribunal for the Former Yugoslavia, the attempts by Servini de Cubría to hold Spain accountable have had important ramifications. For example, the more than twenty men she indicted in 2014 may never be able to leave Spain again or risk extradition to Argentina and face trial for human rights abuses. Much like Pinochet in the late 1990s, these men have effectively been placed under country arrest. Furthermore, as the bodies from these exhumations are reburied, the media will cover it and the country will have to continue to face its past.

International entities such as the United Nations, Amnesty International, and the European Union have increasingly condemned Spain for not addressing the crimes of the Civil War and the Franco regime. Though these institutions have not attempted to do anything substantial, such as imposing sanctions, their criticism of Spain's handling of the past suggests that neighboring countries do not believe the Spanish government's narrative and do not condone how it has handled its violent past. This is also a reflection of the work done by the ARMH, the Spanish historical memory movement, and the Argentinean universal jurisdiction case; the people involved in those groups have all labored hard to spread a reframed collective memory of violence in Spain. Moreover, the use of international law and TANs have helped to support the ideas that crimes against humanity do not have an expiration date on adjudication and that justice is not limited to the perpetrating countries' legal system. Importantly, for future activism, the Spanish case very clearly emboldens civil society groups to continue their grassroots work, even when domestic courts deny them the opportunity to obtain justice.

However small these gains may seem, it is imperative to point out that for the families of the victims in Spain, they are monumental. The "rights of families" frame is entirely contingent on this very idea. Families having the fundamental right to bury their loved ones in accordance with the family's wishes rather than the actions of murders cannot be understated. The ability for families to recover, identify, and rebury their loved ones is one of the clearest and most important aspects of the new models of posttransitional justice. As forensic science and genomic testing continue to progress, the opportunities for families suffering from the aftermath of state terror and violence will hopefully continue to expand so that everyone has the ability to recover and rebury their loved ones with dignity.

Concerning the exhumations in Guadalajara, in early June 2017, the DNA analysis came back with the exciting news that the last person buried in the first plot, and the first exhumed, was Timoteo Mendieta Alcalá. He was reburied on July 2, 2017, surrounded by hundreds of mourners waving Republican flags; the Spanish press attentively covered the funeral. At the funeral, Juan Carlos Mestre read a long and moving poem dedicated to Timoteo and Ascensión. As his casket, draped in a Republican flag, was lowered into the grave, Ascensión threw Republican flag–colored purple, yellow, and red carnations onto his grave (see fig. 5.8), sobbing, "My beloved father, here you are finally. What a shame! My God, what a shame!" She looked around and said, "Thank you all for coming on this sad day." Someone in the back yelled, "Thank you for fighting!" The funeral ended with a string quartet leading the group of mourners in singing "Canto a la Libertad." After the funeral, until she died in September 2019, Ascensión continued to fight for all the assassinated in

FIGURE 5.8 Ascensión with Republican flag–colored flowers at her
father's funeral

the Guadalajara cemetery and the rest of Spain to be exhumed, identified, and reburied by their families. She was buried alongside her father, as per her wishes. Many of those exhumed from the Guadalajara plots have also been reburied in accordance with their family's wishes. Ascensión attended many of these funerals before her passing.

EPILOGUE

s the battle over historical narratives and necropower does not have a finite deadline or objective, we must continue to observe and learn from the various forensics-based human rights movements working across the world. It will also be fascinating to see how these human rights activists—including in Spain—continue to navigate necropolitics and justice efforts in postauthoritarian states through scientific interventions, as well as how the state responds to these endeavors.

Since the time of my fieldwork, the world of Spanish forensics-based human rights has continued to evolve. At the time of this writing, many regional governments, such as those in the Basque and Catalan regions and parts of Andalucía, have decided to take over the responsibility of performing exhumations of Civil War and Franco-era dead. They are coordinating with universities, such as the Basque group Aranzadi that operates out of the University of San Sebastian, or are creating and paying for their own regional teams.

Interestingly, a new socialist government was elected in 2018 and in October 2019 exhumed and reburied the body of Francisco Franco. He is now interred in his family's mausoleum in the El Pardo Cemetery on the outskirts of Madrid. Though the government received intense pushback from right-wing groups who threatened to protest heavily on the day of the exhumation, the event went off without any problems. This may also have been because the state closed all the roads and entrances to both the Valley of the Fallen and El Pardo Cemetery and installed a heavy police presence.

The ARMH, in many ways, has been left behind by the changes in memory politics and forensics-based human rights team developments in Spain. In the last year, due to the association's lack of financial support, poor management, and political infighting, its technical work has become limited. Though the ARMH still carries out small exhumations, perhaps to prove the association is still relevant, it seems to be turning into an advocacy organization focused on calling for more changes in the memory laws throughout the country. Only time will tell what will become of the organization. It has bounced back from similar challenges before.

However, other teams made up entirely of professional scientists and technicians are filling in the gaps. Depending on one's perspective, the increased professionalization or use of true experts, rather than the expertification of citizens, could be either a good or a bad thing. Having citizen experts has contributed to the ARMH's bottom-up effort, as well as empowering many victims' families to directly participate in fighting against Spain's punitive memory politics.

Yet, in spite of the rise of these other teams and the ARMH's seeming decline, it should be noted that many of these new teams are replicating ARMH's tactics of pedagogy, local engagement, and transnational advocacy efforts. In the end, its greatest impact may be larger than the fact that the association originated forensics-based human rights in Spain. Notably, its most important influence could actually be the creation of those truly useful and potent movement tactics that break silences, reframe painful histories of state terror in meaningful ways, and actualize new forms of achievable justice.

The Spanish case speaks not only to the power of state terror but also, importantly, to the power of forensics-based human rights. Though the violence suffered during the Spanish Civil War and Franco regime ended generations ago, the trauma it created did not. Forensics-based human rights have consequently provided human rights workers the tools to help victims' families recover and properly bury their relatives. While closure may only ever be a hope, these families at least have gained a little control over how their loved ones are remembered and cared for in death.

Again, we should remember that the fight against impunity and for remembering the truth of state terror is a worldwide issue. Every day the news uncovers new atrocities: mass killings in Syria, genocide in Myanmar, and discoveries of clandestine mass graves in Iraq. The search for the disappeared and historical truth during episodes of violence and state terror is a familiar plague that has followed humanity into the twenty-first century. However, there is a bright spot. As this book has demonstrated, human rights workers now have the ability to help victims' families recover not only their loved ones but also the truth about their violent deaths, thereby obtaining variations of justice, even eighty years later.

Human rights workers around the world now have the opportunity to expose the often-brutal historical truths of what happened during military regimes, civil wars, and genocide. The power of forensics-based human rights can provide indisputable answers to "What happened?" and "What now?," often in ways that are difficult to ignore, even for state authorities. As this research has shown, well-trained forensic human rights activists can use evidence to unmask state terror and success-fully challenge dominant but distorted historical narratives of past violence. Through forensic-based interventions, dedicated human rights workers such as the members of the ARMH fracture the fear that has silenced historical memory, thereby shattering state-imposed silences. Their work contributes not only to recovering the past, however painful, but also the dignity of the disappeared.

METHODOLOGICAL APPENDIX

SPAIN PARTICIPANT OBSERVATIONS (2015-2017)

My ethnographic fieldwork consisted of observing the daily operations of the ARMH's laboratory in Ponferrada, Spain, attending all feasible public events, and observing and *fully* participating in searches and exhumations of mass graves. The multisited approach to participant observation encouraged my decision to follow the association's actions, which enabled me to be embedded in all of their work and to gain access to all those interacting with the association (Marcus 2009). The multisited ethnographic approach allowed me to observe many different regions of Spain, including Galicia, Castilla-Leon, La Mancha, and Cadiz. Given the political significance of regionalism in Spain, this approach offered the opportunity to view the association's work and impact across a variety of regions and its reception by locals. I selected the ARMH because it was the originator of the movement in Spain and was the most active and recognized organization conducting exhumations during the time I was doing my fieldwork.

I obtained access by contacting the association, who welcomed me to work alongside its workers during the times I requested. In exchange, and in an attempt to engage in feminist ethnographic methodologies, I did volunteer work, as a form of reciprocity, which included organizing and digitizing documents, translating various items, such as American military records, guest books, and reports, working as an English translator at times, and reworking and organizing its database of previous exhumations (Huisman 2008).

While in the field, I took extensive notes in a private notebook. On occasion, I would also record the audio of public events on my tape recorder or access the association's video archive of public events, to further cross-check and add details to my full field notes, which were written for each observation and then hand coded.

CONTENT ANALYSIS

I also conducted two content analyses. The first was an analysis of the seven visitor guest books, where visitors to the exhumations would write their comments and feelings about each of the observed exhumations. I reviewed and coded entries by hand, looking specifically for mentions of artifacts, bones, signs of violence, the classes, history, and science. The second was an analysis of ten news articles covering both the announcement of a reburial and homage event in Villafranca, Spain, and ten articles about the event itself. To obtain my sample, I systematically searched the various local media outlets on Google, Google News, and LexisNexis.

However, only regional and local papers, which are not included in academic news data sites, covered the event. I created the sample from a total of twenty-one articles I found combing through the local newspaper archives. I then read each article, developed a coding scheme, and coded the articles. The coding scheme focused on words used to describe the history of violence, references to Nazi death camps, references to science, and quotations from key actors and whether they made political statements, emotive statements, or references to science or transitional justice. I then analyzed the findings of the codes.

QUALITATIVE INTERVIEWS IN SPAIN

In addition, I conducted two hundred informal interviews with nonactivist Spaniards who either attended mass grave exhumations or other memory events. I also recruited fifteen activists working within the ARMH and fifteen nonactivists to do formal and recorded interviews. I used respondent-driven sampling, or snowball sampling, to recruit the formal interviews of both the activists and nonactivists. I recruited all nonactivists in the area where the ARMH laboratory is located in the northwest Castilla-Leon region of Spain. All but one of the interviewees were aware that the ARMH had a laboratory in their town.

For all the interviews, I designed and followed a semistructured interview guide, which differed slightly depending on whether the respondent was an activist or nonactivist. The activist interview guide covered more about the participant's personal experiences working in human rights. However, I designed both interview guides to focus on the respondents' opinions about the history of political violence in Spain, human rights in general, the memory movement in Spain, the role of exhumations and DNA on human rights, and whether the respondents thought the dominant historical narrative about the past violence was changing and why. The interviews ranged from thirty minutes to two hours.

I conducted the formal interviews in private offices and homes (all of which I recorded, transcribed, and coded). The interviews and transcriptions were done in Spanish. During the data analysis and coding process, I translated key parts of the interviews into English. I coded all of the interviews using the qualitative software HyperResearch. Respondents could choose to be identified by their real name—the preferred option of public figures—or a pseudonym of my choosing. When using real names, I use first and last names; the pseudonyms are only first names. Although the main figures of the association have agreed to be named, I have opted to identify them only by their work titles. When quoting interviews, I have removed all nonessential utterances such as "umm" or "uh-huhs" for clarity.

I carried out the informal interviews in public spaces including graveside during searches and exhumations, and in theaters, cafés, and houses. I realized rather quickly that in these public spaces, even with the promise of confidentiality, the use of a recorder was limiting in terms of access and responses. While recording interviews privately is useful in obtaining more accurate data, I believe that, in this case, the open, informal nature of these interviews was better able to access the respondents' true beliefs due to the taboo nature of the subject. I also believe that it is possible that at times, respondents, when in larger public groups, could have engaged in self-censorship. However, being in a group was rare; I conducted most of the interviews one-on-one in an informal way. As a foreign woman with no direct connection to Spain or its history of violence, I assuaged many of my respondents' fears about my own views of the past. Rather, many respondents often took on a teacher-like role with me in explaining both the history of the violence and their current opinions. My informal interviews functioned more like conversations, which, when appropriate, I would write down while the informants were speaking. Otherwise, I would wait—often no longer than ten minutes—to reconstruct the conversation in my field notes. These interviews were coded by hand. Nonetheless, I was able, in some cases, to record these informal interviews. They were then transcribed and coded. I have removed all identifiable information from the informal interviews to protect the privacy of the respondents.

INTERNATIONAL ORGANIZATIONS INTERVIEWS

I additionally conducted fifty-five interviews with scientists, technicians, and citizen experts working in forensics teams. These teams included the Committee on Missing Persons (CMP) in Cyprus, the International Commission on Missing Persons (ICMP) in Bosnia and Herzegovina, the Argentine Forensic Anthropology Team (EAAF), and a variety of freelance forensics-based human rights scientists working in Canada and Spain. As with the other interviews I followed a semistructured interview guide that used many of the same questions posed to activist Spaniards yet differed in that many more questions focused on their roles as scientists, their beliefs about the role of science in human rights, the role of their organization in human rights, and scientific protocols and networks.

POSITIONALITY AND REFLEXIVITY

I tried to engage with reflexivity, or the process of looking both inward and outward in regard to the positionality of my research and my research process, in all the spaces I occupied as a foreign woman coming from a prestigious American university (Ahmed, Hundt, and Blackburn 2011; Huisman 2008; Shaw and Gould 2001). Being a foreign woman from a high-status university undoubtedly affected the setting and interactions I had with my interlocutors. I found that being a foreign woman, with no perceivable family ties to Spain or the Spanish Civil War, in spite of my Basque last name, was useful in the field. My university credentials, in addition to being from California—a distant but well-revered place—also lent me a certain amount of credibility, which seemed to help me gain access.

I also found that being a foreign woman in the field had both its benefits and downsides. Being foreign certainly afforded me a certain level of interest and access that I would not have had if I had been from Spain. However, the flip side of that was that sometimes I received more attention than I wanted. Like other female researchers, I found that my gender encouraged female interviewees to be more open and willing to share their experiences (Riessman 1994). I also found that my gender would sometimes prevent men from sharing more explicit accounts of violence or gendered violence for fear of upsetting my sensibilities.

NOTES

INTRODUCTION

1. There is a wonderful, and extensive, world of scholarly literature on the Spanish case that informs my analysis, and which it builds off of, including work that ranges in focus from understanding the necropolitics of Franco and his regime (Ferrándiz 2020; de Menezes 2018) to its transition to democracy (Aguilar and Fernández 2002; Golob 2008), the failings of the democratic transition (Hajji 2014; Kovras 2013; Magaldi Fernández 2019), the memory movement's origins (Ferrándiz 2013; Renshaw 2011; Silva 2005), and its impact (Bevernage and Colaert 2014; Ferrándiz 2008; Graham 2004; de Mata 2009; de Mata 2007; Rubin 2018). There is also a growing literature on the role of archaeology in understanding the Spanish Civil War and the Franco regime (Gelonch-Solé 2013; Renshaw 2010), the role of scientific discovery in exhumations and forensic work (Anon 2004; Eduardo Penedo et al. 2009; Etxeberria and Serrulla 2020; Etxeberria, Serrulla, Fernando, and Herrasti 2014; Gabilondo 2012; Gelonch-Solé 2013; González-Ruibal 2011, 2012; Gutiérrez 2009; Prieto 2008; Rech 2018; Ruibal 2008), the impact of early exhumations (Aguilar and Fernández 2002; Ferrándiz 2016; Ferrándiz Martín 2007), the impact of exhumations today (Ferrándiz 2020; Gil and de Pablos 2020; Rubin 2015, 2016), their impact on judicial understandings of the past (Rubin 2018), and cultural representations of the violence (Ferrándiz 2014, 2016; Labanyi 2006, 2007; Rubin 2020). It is also inevitable when writing a book about forensics-based human rights that there is overlap with others in the description

of behaviors, such as how forensic technicians perform their work, or specifically in the case of the ARMH, how they use pedagogy during mass exhumations to teach the locals about the "true" history of the violence (Colaert 2016; Colaert 2015; Ferrándiz 2016; Renshaw 2011; Rubin 2015). My work builds on the previous observations of others to foster a contextualization of these actions within a global movement and unpack their impact at multiple levels. Moreover, my analysis looks at these tactics as being part of a reconceptualized definition of justice, rather than solely being an effective movement tactic or example of memory politics (Colaert 2016; Colaert, Lore 2015; Ferrándiz 2008, 2013, 2016; Renshaw 2010, 2011; Rubin 2020).

2. Ironically, the first example of a large-scale forensic investigation into mass killings was the Nazi-backed exhumation of twenty-two thousand executed Polish soldiers in the Russian Katyn forest in the early 1940s. The Nazis conducted this investigation to protect themselves against culpability for the massacre. The Germans meticulously documented their exhumation and study of over four thousand human remains; they concluded that the occupying Soviet forces had summarily executed the deceased. Other reevaluations of their work have confirmed these results (Rosenblatt 2015; Schwartz 1993; Zawodny 2015). During the postwar military tribunals, the Soviet government tried to include this massacre as part of the charges against Nazi officials, but the case was thrown out due to precise scientific findings of the Nazis' forensic investigations (Rosenblatt 2015: 34).

3. Specifically, the forensic turn is the idea that science, such as forensic anthropology, can be used to investigate and "establish facts in a court of law" (Colaert 2016; Colaert, 2015; Dziuban 2017), whereas the "forensic cascade," based on Kathryn Sikkink's (2011) idea that the increase in human rights prosecutions in transitional settings has created a cascade like effect, encourages more and more justice interventions in cases of human rights abuses (Sikkink 2011).

4. This number is contested, but it is the number most commonly used by major human rights organizations in Argentina.

5. Not all the Mothers groups were supportive of exhumations; some were vehemently against them, fearing that by acknowledging the deaths of their children the government could move on without being held accountable or telling the full truth of the past (Rosenblatt 2015).

6. This is also when the forensic turn fully intersected memory politics, as forensics in this case was focused around the "right to the truth" (Dziuban 2017; Rosenblatt 2015). This book further demonstrates that the truth generated by forensic interventions may be the most tangible form of achievable justice in cases of long-ago violence or countries with amnesty laws.

7. Forensic archeologists also (depending on their resources) use ground-penetrating radar, satellite, or aerial photography to help in their work.

8. These protocols cover exhumations and autopsy procedures while acknowledging that many factors may impact investigations including lack of resources, poor conditions, and the sociocultural and religious differences that can make this kind of work both unwanted and taboo (Rosenblatt 2015).

9. In the beginning of forensics-based human rights, the protocols were shaped by local constraints, such as the amnesty laws in Latin America (Kovras 2017: 98). The "family-centric model" approach, used by both the EAAF and the ARMH, includes working closely with the victim's family organizations and placing a high value on identification and reburial, which they framed as a basic human right (Rosenblatt 2015). This can get complicated when bodies are difficult or impossible to identify, a challenge faced by all teams, as not all remains are conserved the same way, making identification possible, and there may be no surviving family members. The impact of the lack of identification is discussed more fully in chapter 5.

10. However, this is not to suggest that their work is not without struggles. Rather, many teams like the ARMH face many difficulties in the field. Across cases, teams face issues in finding graves, getting willing witnesses to help locate graves, difficult terrains and field sites, as well as, depending on the sociopolitical situations on the ground, issues with personal safety (Azevedo 2016; Kovras 2013, 2017; Rosenblatt 2015; Sanford 2003; Wagner 2008). For example, not everyone is going to be happy about the return of the disappeared. In some cases, such as in Guatemala, Bosnia and Herzegovina, and Indonesia, the perpetrators are still alive and not always thrilled at the idea of being held accountable. Additionally, in some cases there can be tensions among the forensic teams, the families, and local memory politics (see Kovras 2017; Rosenblatt 2015). In Spain, due to the length of time that has passed, the threat of dealing with perpetrators is increasingly less likely. Rather, the main issues the ARMH

faces is difficulty in finding the graves due to changing topographies, and combating the pervasive belief, pushed by the Franco regime and the democratic transition, that the past is best left in the past and that any kind of effort to address it will open old wounds. The ARMH does try to combat this through a variety of tactics including inviting locals to participate in the search for graves and asking for testimonies, as well as teaching forensics and history courses at their mass grave exhumations. These tactics are by no means only used by the ARMH, as they have been successfully deployed in Central and South America, as well as by other Spanish forensic teams. ARMH responses to these challenges will be covered in more detail in chapter 3.

11. This book is thus not about the functioning of science and technology, but rather how forensics and DNA testing are tools for the construction of historical memory and transitional justice politics.

12. Many quotes in this book are from confidential sources; to protect their anonymity, I have not provided any identifying details and all names provided, unless the participants agreed to be identified or are public figures, are pseudonyms.

1. *NO PASARÁN?* THE SPANISH CIVIL WAR, THE FRANCO REGIME, AND DEMOCRACY

1. I use this term as it is the common phrasing of the political situation of the region. Its use does not condone colonialism or occupation.

2. England eventually allowed General Pinochet to return to Chile in March 2000, after it was allegedly established that he was suffering from dementia and was unable to physically withstand extradition. He lived for another six years. He died peacefully in his bed surrounded by his family and was never legally held accountable for the violence of his regime.

2. EXCAVATIONS: A SCIENTIFIC TROJAN HORSE

1. The ARMH, and any forensics team, must have official permissions from the local government if the suspected burial site is on public land and permission from private landowners. Private landowners have been known to demand money for permission to excavate, while others have pulled their permission in the middle of the work.

2. His willingness to help was most likely bolstered by the knowledge that his participation would not harm him due to the amnesty laws.

3. AT THE FOOT OF THE GRAVE: TEACHING SCIENCE AND THE "TRUE" HISTORY OF SPAIN

1. I use the word "classes" because the ARMH itself calls these interactions *classes en el pie de la fosa*, or "classes at the foot of the grave."
2. In traditional Catholic cemeteries, the graveyard is normally segregated between consecrated ground and the civil part of the cemetery, which holds the remains of suicides, unbaptized babies, and non-Catholics.

4. REBURYING THE DEAD: PERFORMANCE OF GRIEF AND REFRAMED NARRATIVES

1. Francisco Franco remained at the Valley of the Fallen until October 24, 2019, when he was exhumed and reburied in the municipal cemetery in El Pardo.
2. For more on the methodology of this section, please see the methodological appendix.
3. He is still, as of this writing, the mayor.
4. Their criminal status, however, remains listed on official government records.
5. The song was originally composed by José Antonio Labordeta in 1975, the same year that Franco died, and the democratic transition began.
6. The local memory association was already aware of the DNA testing problems.
7. Pedro Guerra wrote "Huesos" in 2004; he dedicated the song to all the Spaniards buried in mass graves who died in the war and during the Franco regime.
8. These trees were later set on fire in an act of vandalism; the local memory association replanted them.

5. TRANSNATIONAL NETWORKS

1. Scholars widely debate how to best implement these ideas and whether or not they can be mutually achieved. Please see Jelin 2007; Kovras 2017; Langer 2011; Pradhan 2020; and Wilson 1999.

2. For more on analysis on La Querella Argentina, and how it relates to international movements, legal understandings of universal jurisdiction, and its impact, please see Druliolle 2020; Hepworth 2020; Langer 2011, 2015; Langer and Eason 2019; and Montoto Ugarte 2014, 2019, 2020.

3. The bodies theoretically correspond with the cemetery ledger, though not always the case, as with Timoteo.

4. European trade unions are known for actively participating in transnational advocacy among progressive causes.

5. In late 2017, the Catalan region voted to secede from Spain. In response, the state revoked its regional sovereignty and held a snap election in December, which diminished the secessionists' power but did not completely remove their prominence in the regional parliament. The Spanish government then arrested a majority of the major secessionist politicians, with the previous leader, Carles Puigdemont, fleeing to Belgium in exile. In 2019, nine of the secessionists were given a range of sentences; some were fined or banned from public office, and some were given up to thirteen years in prison for treason and secessionism (Jones and Burgen 2019).

BIBLIOGRAPHY

Aguilar, Paloma. 2008. "Transitional or Post-Transitional Justice? Recent Developments in the Spanish Case." *South European Society and Politics* 13(4): 417–33.

Aguilar, Paloma. 2017. "Unwilling to Forget: Local Memory Initiatives in Post-Franco Spain." *South European Society and Politics* 22(4): 405–26.

Aguilar, Paloma, and Paloma Aguilar Fernández. 2002. *Memory and Amnesia: The Role of the Spanish Civil War in the Transition to Democracy.* Oxford: Berghahn.

Ahmed, Dunya Ahmed Abdulla, Gillian Lewando Hundt, and Clare Blackburn. 2011. "Issues of Gender, Reflexivity and Positionality in the Field of Disability: Researching Visual Impairment in an Arab Society." *Qualitative Social Work* 10(4): 467–84.

Akrich, Madeleine, and Bruno Latour. 1992. *A Summary of a Convenient Vocabulary for the Semiotics of Human and Nonhuman Assemblies.* Cambridge, MA: MIT Press.

Albright, Madeleine. 2019. *Fascism: A Warning.* New York: HarperPerennial.

Anon. 1969. *Ley 62/1969, de 22 de Julio, Por La Que Se Provee Lo Concerniente a La Sucesión En La Jefatura Del Estado.*

Anon. 2007. *Boletín Oficial Del Estado. 2007. LEY 52/2007.*

Anon. 2008. *La Actuación de la Audiencia Nacional en la Investigación y Juicio de los Crímenes Contra La Humanidad Cometidos en la Guerra Civil y El Franquismo: Del Auto de 16 de Octubre a La Decisión Del Pleno de la Sala de Lo Penal de 2 de Diciembre de 2008 Congress.*

Anon. n.d. *La Ley 46/1977, de 15 De Octubre, de Amnistía, Article Boletín Oficial del Estado (1977).*

Arditti, Rita. 2002. "The Grandmothers of the Plaza De Mayo and the Struggle against Impunity in Argentina." *Meridians: Feminism, Race, Transnationalism* 3(1): 19–41.

Armengou, Montse, Ricard Belis, and Ricard Vinyes. 2002. *Los Niños Perdidos Del Franquismo*. Televisió de Catalunya.

Armstrong, Elizabeth A., and Suzanna M. Crage. 2006. "Movements and Memory: The Making of the Stonewall Myth." *American Sociological Review* 71(5): 724–51.

Ashplant, Timothy G., Graham Dawson, and Michael Roper. 2000. "The Politics of War Memory and Commemoration." *Psychology Press* 7.

Azevedo, Valérie Robin. 2016. "Restoring the Dignity of the Wars Disappeared? Exhumations of Mass Graves, Restorative Justice and Compassion Policies in Peru." *Human Remains and Violence: An Interdisciplinary Journal* 2(2): 39–55.

Bachiller, Carmen. 2018. "Ascensión Mendieta, Víctima Del Franquismo y La Abogada Ana Messuti, 'Premio Memoria Histórica.'" *El Diario*, April 4.

Badcock, James. 2016. "Spain Franco: Victim's Daughter Praises Open Past." *BBC*.

Badcock, James. 2017. "Franco Victim's Body Exhumed for Dignified Burial After 75-Year Battle." *The Telegraph*, July 1.

Banjeglav, Tamara. 2013. "Conflicting Memories, Competing Narratives and Contested Histories in Croatia's Post-War Commemorative Practices." *Politička Misao: Časopis Za Politologiju* 49(5): 7–31.

Beck, Ulrich. 1992. *Risk Society: Towards a New Modernity*. London: Sage.

Benford, Robert D., and David A. Snow. 2000. "Framing Processes and Social Movements: An Overview and Assessment." *Annual Review of Sociology* 26(1): 611–39.

Berger, Ronald. 2003. "It Ain't Necessarily So: The Politics of Memory and the Bystander Narrative in the US Holocaust Memorial Museum." *Humanity & Society* 27(1): 6–29.

Bernardi, Patricia, and Luis Fondebrider. 2007. "Forensic Archaeology and the Scientific Documentation of Human Rights Violations: An Argentinian Example from the Early 1980s." *Forensic Archaeology and Human Rights Violations* 205: 32.

Bevernage, Berber, and Lore Colaert. 2014. "History from the Grave? Politics of Time in Spanish Mass Grave Exhumations." *Memory Studies* 7(4): 440–56.

Blau, Soren, and Mark Skinner. 2005. "The Use of Forensic Archaeology in the Investigation of Human Rights Abuse: Unearthing the Past in East Timor." *The International Journal of Human Rights* 9(4): 449–63.

Bodnar, John. 1992. *Remaking America: Public Memory, Commemoration, and Patriotism in the Twentieth Century*. Princeton, NJ: Princeton University Press.

Bosco, Fernando J. 2004. "Human Rights Politics and Scaled Performances of Memory: Conflicts among the Madres de Plaza de Mayo in Argentina." *Social & Cultural Geography* 5(3): 381–402.

Bourdieu, Pierre. 1986. "The Force of Law: Toward a Sociology of the Juridical Field." *Hastings Law Journal* 38: 805.

Bourdieu, Pierre. 2004. "From the King's House to the Reason of State: A Model of the Genesis of the Bureaucratic Field." *Constellations* 11(1): 16–36.

Bouvard, Marguerite Guzman. 2002. *Revolutionizing Motherhood: The Mothers of the Plaza de Mayo*. Lanham, MD: Rowman & Littlefield.

Bruce, Katherine McFarland. 2013. "LGBT Pride as a Cultural Protest Tactic in a Southern City." *Journal of Contemporary Ethnography* 42(5): 608–35.

Burbidge, Peter. 2011. "Waking the Dead of the Spanish Civil War: Judge Baltasar Garzón and the Spanish Law of Historical Memory." *Journal of International Criminal Justice* 9(3): 753–81.

Burchianti, Margaret E. 2004. "Building Bridges of Memory: The Mothers of the Plaza de Mayo and the Cultural Politics of Maternal Memories." *History and Anthropology* 15(2): 133–50.

Burns, Karen Ramey. 2015. *Forensic Anthropology Training Manual*. New York: Routledge.

Butler, Judith, and Athena Athanasiou. 2013. *Dispossession: The Performative in the Political*. New York: Wiley.

Cabrero, Olga. 2014. *Guide to Legal Research in Spain*. GlobaLex website.

Camargo Jr, Kenneth, and Roy Grant. 2015. "Public Health, Science, and Policy Debate: Being Right Is Not Enough." *American Journal of Public Health* 105(2): 232–35.

Carracedo, Ángel, and Lourdes Prieto. 2019. "Beyond the CSI Effect." *Métode Science Studies Journal* (9): 31–37.

Cassia, Paul Sant. 2005. *Bodies of Evidence: Burial, Memory and the Recovery of Missing Persons in Cyprus*. Vol. 20. Oxford: Berghahn.

Cech, Erin A., and Heidi M. Sherick. 2015. "Depoliticization and the Structure of Engineering Education." Pp. 203–16 in *International Perspectives on Engineering Education*. New York: Springer.

Cerulo, Karen A. 1993. "Symbols and the World System: National Anthems and Flags." *Sociological Forum* 8(2): 243–71.

Colaert, Lore. 2015. "History from the Grave: Politics of Memory in Exhumations of Mass Graves from the Spanish Civil War." PhD thesis, Ghent University.

Colaert, Lore. 2016. "Excavating a Hidden Past: The Forensic Turn in Spain's Collective Memory." Pp. 336–56 in *Excavating Memory: Sites of Remembering and Forgetting*, ed. Maria Theresia Starzmann and John R. Roby. Gainesville: University Press of Florida.

Colangelo, Anthony J. 2021. "Germany Used 'Universal Jurisdiction' to Convict Ex-Syrian Official Who Sent Protestors to Torture Camp." *InsideSources*. Retrieved April 5, 2021, https://insidesources.com/germany-used-universal -jurisdiction-to-convict-ex-syrian-official-who-sent-protestors-to-torture -camp/.

Cole, Simon A. 2009. *Suspect Identities: A History of Fingerprinting and Criminal Identification*. Cambridge, MA: Harvard University Press.

Congram, Derek, and Jon Sterenberg. 2009. "Grave Challenges in Iraq." Pp. 441–53 in *Handbook of Forensic Anthropology and Archaeology*, ed. Soren Blau and Douglas H. Ubelaker. New York: Routledge.

Crossland, Zoe. 2013. "Evidential Regimes of Forensic Archaeology." *Annual Review of Anthropology* 42: 121–37.

·Davis, Madeleine. 2005. "Is Spain Recovering Its Memory? Breaking the 'Pacto Del Olvido.'" *Human Rights Quarterly* 858–80.

De León, Jason. 2015. *The Land of Open Graves: Living and Dying on the Migrant Trail*. Vol. 36. University of California Press.

Donnelly, Sarah. 2012. "Forensic Science in a Human Rights Framework." *Australian Journal of Forensic Sciences* 44(1): 93–103.

Doretti, Mercedes, and Clyde C. Snow. 2003. "Forensic Anthropology and Human Rights." *Hard Evidence: Case Studies in Forensic Anthropology* 290.

Dowsett, Sonya. Febuary 10, 2016. "Spanish Civil War Graves Exhumed." *Reuters*, https://widerimage.reuters.com/story/spain-civil-war-graves-exhumed.

Drawdy, Shuala M., and Cheryl Katzmarzyk. 2016. "The Missing Files: The Experience of the International Committee of the Red Cross." Pp. 60–73 in *Missing Persons: Multidisciplinary Perspectives on the Disappeared*, ed. Derek Congram. Toronto: Canadian Scholar's Press.

Druliolle, Vincent. 2020. "Movilización Legal." *EUNOMÍA. Revista En Cultura de La Legalidad* (19): 365–74.

Duterme, Clara. 2016. "Honouring, Commemorating, Compensating: State and Civil Society in Response to Victims of the Armed Conflict in the Ixil Region (Guatemala)." *Human Remains and Violence: An Interdisciplinary Journal* 2(2): 3–20.

Dziuban, Zuzanna. 2017. *Mapping the "Forensic Turn": Engagements with Materialities of Mass Death in Holocaust Studies and Beyond.* Vienna: New Academic Press.

Eduardo Penedo, Juan Sanguino, Francisco Etxeberria, Lourdes Herrasti, Antxon Bandres, and Claudio Albisu. 2009. "Restos Humanos Del Frente Del Jarama En La Guerra Civil 1936–1939." *Munibe Antropologia-Arkeologia* 60.

Encarnación, Omar G. 2007. "Pinochet's Revenge: Spain Revisits Its Civil War." *World Policy Journal* 24(4): 39–50.

Encarnación, Omar G. 2008. "Reconciliation After Democratization: Coping with the Past in Spain." *Political Science Quarterly* 123(3): 435–59.

Encarnación, Omar G. 2014. *Democracy Without Justice in Spain: The Politics of Forgetting.* College Station: University of Pennsylvania Press

Epstein, Steven. 1996. *Impure Science: AIDS, Activism, and the Politics of Knowledge.* Vol. 7. Berkeley: University of California Press.

Etxeberria, Francisco, and Fernando Serrulla. 2020. "The Case of the Brains of La Pedraja: Forensic Sciences and Historical Memory in Spain." *Mètode Science Studies Journal: Annual Review* (10): 109–17.

Etxeberria, Francisco, Serrulla, Fernando, and Lourdes Herrasti. 2014. "Simas, Cavernas y Pozos Para Ocultar Cadáveres En La Guerra Civil Española (1936–1939). Aportaciones Desde La Antropología Forense." *Munibe* 65.

Eyal, Gil. 2013. "For a Sociology of Expertise: The Social Origins of the Autism Epidemic." *American Journal of Sociology* 118(4): 863–907.

Feitlowitz, Marguerite. 2011. *A Lexicon of Terror: Argentina and the Legacies of Torture, Revised and Updated with a New Epilogue.* Oxford: Oxford University Press.

Ferllini, R. F. 1997. "Rwanda: Political Conflict and Genocide." *Torture* 7(3): 72–76.

Ferrándiz, Francisco. 2008. "Cries and Whispers: Exhuming and Narrating Defeat in Spain Today." *Journal of Spanish Cultural Studies* 9(2): 177–92.

Ferrándiz, Francisco. 2013. "Exhuming the Defeated: Civil War Mass Graves in 21st-Century Spain." *American Ethnologist* 40(1): 38–54.

Ferrándiz, Francisco. 2014. *El Pasado Bajo Tierra: Exhumaciones Contemporáneas de La Guerra Civil.* Barcelona: Anthropos.

Ferrándiz, Francisco and Antonius C. G. M. Robben, ed. 2015. *Necropolitics: Mass Graves and Exhumations in the Age of Human Rights*. Philadelphia: University of Pennsylvania Press.

Ferrándiz, Francisco. 2016. "Afterlives: A Social Autopsy of Mass Grave Exhumations in Spain." Pp. 41–61 in *Legacies of Violence in Contemporary Spain*, ed. Ofelia Ferrán and Lisa Hilbink. New York: Routledge.

Ferrándiz, Francisco. 2020. "Transacciones Necropolíticas En La España Contemporánea. Fosas Comunes, Generales Golpistas y Mausoleos En El Aire." *Mélanges de La Casa de Velázquez. Nouvelle Série* (50–1): 301–4.

Ferrándiz Martín, Francisco. 2007. "Exhumaciones y Políticas de La Memoria En La España Contemporánea." *Hispania Nova* 7: 621–40

Fine, Gary Alan. 1995. "Public Narration and Group Culture: Discerning Discourse in Social Movements." *Social Movements and Culture* 4: 127–43.

Fondebrider, Luis. 2002. "Reflections on the Scientific Documentation of Human Rights Violations." *International Review of the Red Cross* 84(848): 885–91.

Fonseret, Roque Moreno, and Virgilio Francisco Candela Sevila. 2018. "Amnistía y (Des) Memoria En La Transición Española." *el@ tina. Revista electrónica de estudios latinoamericanos* 16(64): 49–61.

Frayer, Lauren. 2016. "Finding a Long-Lost Father as Spain Exhumes Decades-Old Mass Graves." *NPR*, February 26.

Gabilondo, Francisco Etxeberria. 2004. "Panorama Organizativo Sobre Antropología y Patología Forense En España. Algunas Propuestas Para El Estudio de Fosas Con Restos Humanos de La Guerra Civil Española de 1936." Pp. 183–219 in *La memoria de los olvidados: un debate sobre el silencio de la represión franquista*. Ámbito.

Gabilondo, Etxeberria. 2012. "Exhumaciones Contemporáneas en España: Las Fosas Comunes de La Guerra Civil." *Boletín Galego de Medicina Legal e Forense* 18: 13–28.

Gamson, Joshua. 2018. " 'The Place That Holds Our Stories': The National AIDS Memorial Grove and Flexible Collective Memory Work." *Social Problems* 65(1): 33–50.

Gandsman, Ari. 2009a. " 'A Prick of a Needle Can Do No Harm': Compulsory Extraction of Blood in the Search for the Children of Argentina's Disappeared." *The Journal of Latin American and Caribbean Anthropology* 14(1): 162–84.

Gandsman, Ari. 2009b. " 'Do You Know Who You Are?' Radical Existential Doubt and Scientific Certainty in the Search for the Kidnapped Children of the Disappeared in Argentina." *Ethos* 37(4): 441–65.

Gauchat, Gordon. 2012. "Politicization of Science in the Public Sphere: A Study of Public Trust in the United States, 1974 to 2010." *American Sociological Review* 77(2): 167–87.

Gell, Alfred. 1998. *Art and Agency: An Anthropological Theory*. Oxford: Clarendon Press.

Gelonch-Solé, Josep. 2013. "Mass Graves from the Civil War and the Franco Era in Spain: Once Forgotten, Now at the Heart of the Public Debate." *European Review* 21(4): 507–22.

Gil, Amalia Pérez-Juez, and Jorge Morín de Pablos. 2020. *Arqueología de La Guerra Civil y La Dictadura Española: La Historia NO Escrita*. Oxford: BAR Publishing.

Goffman, Erving. 1974. *Frame Analysis: An Essay on the Organization of Experience*. Cambridge, MA: Harvard University Press.

Goffman, Erving. 2009. *Stigma: Notes on the Management of Spoiled Identity*. New York: Simon & Schuster.

Goldenberg, Myrna. 1996. "Lessons Learned from Gentle Heroism: Women's Holocaust Narratives." *The Annals of the American Academy of Political and Social Science* 548(1): 78–93.

Golob, Stephanie R. 2008. "Volver: The Return of/to Transitional Justice Politics in Spain." *Journal of Spanish Cultural Studies* 9(2): 127–41.

González-Ruibal, Alfredo. 2011. "Digging Franco's Trenches: An Archaeological Investigation of a Nationalist Position from the Spanish Civil War." *Journal of Conflict Archaeology* 6(2): 97–123.

González-Ruibal, Alfredo. 2012. "From the Battlefield to the Labour Camp: Archaeology of Civil War and Dictatorship in Spain." *Antiquity* 86(332): 456–73.

González-Ruibal, Alfredo, and Carmen Ortiz García. 2015. *The Prison of Carabanchel (Madrid, Spain): A Life Story*. Cambridge: Cambridge University Press.

Graham, Helen. 2004. "The Spanish Civil War, 1936–2003: The Return of Republican Memory." *Science & Society* 68(3: Special issue): 313–28.

Graham, Helen. 2005. *The Spanish Civil War: A Very Short Introduction*. Vol. 123. Oxford: Oxford University Press.

De Grazia, Victoria. 1992. *How Fascism Ruled Women: Italy, 1922–1945.* Berkeley: University of California Press.

Griswold, Wendy, Gemma Mangione, and Terence E. McDonnell. 2013. "Objects, Words, and Bodies in Space: Bringing Materiality into Cultural Analysis." *Qualitative Sociology* 36(4): 343–64.

Grotius, Hugo. 2005. "The Rights of War and Peace, Ed." *Richard Tuck (Indianapolis: Liberty Fund, 2005)* 393(1186): 1–21.

Gutiérrez, J. Montero. 2009. "La Visibilidad Arqueológica de Un Conflicto Inconcluso: La Exhumación de Fosas Comunes de La Guerra Civil Española a Debate." *Munibe Antropologia-Arkeologia* 60: 289–308.

Habermas, Jürgen, and Marc Buhot de Launay. 1978. *L'espace public: Archéologie de la publicité comme dimension constitutive de la société bourgeoise.* Paris: Payot.

Haglund, William D., Melissa Connor, and Douglas D. Scott. 2001. "The Archaeology of Contemporary Mass Graves." *Historical Archaeology* 35(1):57–69.

Hajji, Nadia. 2014. "Post-Transitional Justice in Spain: Passing the Historic Memory Law." PhD thesis, Duke University.

Hamilton, Lawrence C., Joel Hartter, and Kei Saito. 2015. "Trust in Scientists on Climate Change and Vaccines." *Sage Open* 5(3): 2158244015602752.

Hepworth, Andrea. 2020. "Memory Activism Across Borders." *Agency in Transnational Memory Politics* 4: 92.

Herman, Judith L. 2015. *Trauma and Recovery: The Aftermath of Violence–from Domestic Abuse to Political Terror.* London: Hachette.

Hertz, Robert. 2017. "A Contribution to the Study of the Collective Representation of Death." Pp. 19–33 in *Death, Mourning, and Burial: A Cross-Cultural Reader*, ed. Antonius C. G. M. Robben. New York: Wiley.

Hindmarsh, R., & Prainsack, B. (Eds.). (2010). *Genetic suspects: Global governance of forensic DNA profiling and databasing.* Cambridge University Press.

Hirsch, Marianne. 2008. "The Generation of Postmemory." *Poetics Today* 29(1): 103–28.

Hochschild, Adam. 2016. *Spain in Our Hearts: Americans in the Spanish Civil War, 1936–1939.* Boston: Houghton Mifflin Harcourt.

Huisman, Kimberly. 2008. " 'Does This Mean You're Not Going to Come Visit Me Anymore?': An Inquiry into an Ethics of Reciprocity and Positionality in Feminist Ethnographic Research." *Sociological Inquiry* 78(3): 372–96.

ICCPED (International Convention for the Protection of All Persons from Enforced Disappearance). 2006. *UN International Convention on Protection of All Persons from Disappearance.* Geneva: OHCHR.

Irvine, William D. 1996. "Domestic Politics and the Fall of France in 1940." *Historical Reflections/Réflexions Historiques* 77–90.

Iturriaga, Nicole. 2019. "The Evolution of the Grandmothers of Plaza de Mayo's Mnemonic Framing." *Mobilization: An International Quarterly* 24(4): 475–92.

Jackson, Gabriel. 2004. "Multiple Historical Meanings of the Spanish Civil War." *Science & Society* 68(3: Special issue): 272–76.

Jasanoff, Sheila. 2004. *States of Knowledge: The Co-Production of Science and the Social Order.* New York: Routledge.

Jelin, Elizabeth. 2003. *State Repression and the Labors of Memory.* Vol. 18. Minneapolis: University of Minnesota Press.

Jelin, Elizabeth. 2007. "Public Memorialization in Perspective: Truth, Justice and Memory of Past Repression in the Southern Cone of South America." *The International Journal of Transitional Justice* 1(1): 138–56.

Jelin, Elizabeth, and Susana G. Kaufman. 2017. "Layers of Memories: Twenty Years After in Argentina." Pp. 89–110 in *Commemorating War,* ed. Timothy G. Ashplant and Michael Roper. New York: Routledge.

Jones, Sam, and Stephen Burgen. 2019. "Violent Clashes over Catalan Separatist Leaders' Prison Terms." *The Guardian,* October 14.

Joyce, Christopher, and Eric Stover. 1991. *Witnesses from the Grave: The Stories Bones Tell.* Boston, MA: Little, Brown.

Juhl, Kirsten. 2005. *The Contribution by (Forensic) Archaeologists to Human Rights Investigations of Mass Graves.* Museum of Archaeology, Stavanger, Norway.

Junquera, Natalia. 2014. "María Martín, una anciana ante las togas." *El País,* July 25.

Keck, Margaret E., and Kathryn Sikkink. 2014. *Activists Beyond Borders: Advocacy Networks in International Politics.* Ithaca, NY: Cornell University Press.

Kellermann, Natan PF. 2001. "The Long-Term Psychological Effects and Treatment of Holocaust Trauma." *Journal of Loss & Trauma* 6(3): 197–218.

Khagram, Sanjeev, James V. Riker, and Kathryn Sikkink. 2002. *Restructuring World Politics: Transnational Social Movements, Networks, and Norms.* Minneapolis: University of Minnesota Press.

King, Richard H. 1996. *Civil Rights and the Idea of Freedom.* Athens: University of Georgia Press.

Kirschner, Robert H., and Karl E. Hannibal. 1994. "The Application of the Forensic Sciences to Human Rights Investigations." *Medicine & Law* 13:451.

Kligman, Gail. 1988. *The Wedding of the Dead: Ritual, Poetics, and Popular Culture in Transylvania*. Vol. 4. Berkeley: University of California Press.

Kolker, Emily S. 2004. "Framing as a Cultural Resource in Health Social Movements: Funding Activism and the Breast Cancer Movement in the US 1990–1993." *Sociology of Health & Illness* 26(6): 820–44.

Kovras, Iosif. 2013. "Explaining Prolonged Silences in Transitional Justice: The Disappeared in Cyprus and Spain." *Comparative Political Studies* 46(6): 730–56.

Kovras, Iosif. 2017. *Grassroots Activism and the Evolution of Transitional Justice: The Families of the Disappeared*. Cambridge: Cambridge University Press.

Kruse, Corinna. 2015. *The Social Life of Forensic Evidence*. Berkeley: University of California Press.

Labanyi, Jo. 2006. "Historias de Víctimas: La Memoria Histórica y El Testimonio En La España Contemporánea." *Iberoamericana (2001–)* 6(24): 87–98.

Labanyi, Jo. 2007. "Memory and Modernity in Democractic Spain: The Difficulty of Coming to Terms with the Spanish Civil War." *Poetics Today* 28(1): 89–116.

Lagunas, Angela Cenarro. 2017. "La Falange Es Un Modo de Ser (Mujer): Discursos e Identidades de Género En Las Publicaciones de La Sección Femenina (1938–1945)." *Historia y Política: Ideas, Procesos y Movimientos Sociales* (37): 91–120.

Lamont, Michèle. 1992. *Money, Morals, and Manners: The Culture of the French and the American Upper-Middle Class*. Chicago: University of Chicago Press.

Lamont, Michèle, and Virág Molnár. 2002. "The Study of Boundaries in the Social Sciences." *Annual Review of Sociology* 28(1): 167–95.

Langer, Máximo. 2011. "The Diplomacy of Universal Jurisdiction: The Political Branches and the Transnational Prosecution of International Crimes." *American Journal of International Law* 105(1): 1–49.

Langer, Máximo. 2015. "Universal Jurisdiction Is Not Disappearing: The Shift from 'Global Enforcer' to 'No Safe Haven' Universal Jurisdiction." *Journal of International Criminal Justice* 13(2): 245–56.

Langer, Maximo, and Mackenzie Eason. 2019. "The Quiet Expansion of Universal Jurisdiction." *European Journal of International Law* 30(3): 779–817.

Latour, Bruno. 1987. *Science in Action: How to Follow Scientists and Engineers Through Society.* Cambridge, MA: Harvard University Press.

Lawless, Christopher. 2013. "The Low Template DNA Profiling Controversy: Biolegality and Boundary Work among Forensic Scientists." *Social Studies of Science* 43(2): 191–214.

Lawless, Christopher. 2016. *Forensic Science: A Sociological Introduction.* New York: Routledge.

Levy, Daniel, and Natan Sznaider. 2010. *Human Rights and Memory.* University Park: Penn State University Press.

Lewandowsky, Stephan, and Klaus Oberauer. 2016. "Motivated Rejection of Science." *Current Directions in Psychological Science* 25(4): 217–22.

Luhmann, N. 1979. *Trust and Power.* New York: Wiley.

Lynch, Michael. 2013. "Science, Truth, and Forensic Cultures: The Exceptional Legal Status of DNA Evidence." *Studies in History and Philosophy of Science Part C: Studies in History and Philosophy of Biological and Biomedical Sciences* 44(1): 60–70.

Lynch, Michael, and Simon A. Cole. 2005. "Science and Technology Studies on Trial: Dilemmas of Expertise." *Social Studies of Science* 35(2): 269–311.

Lynch, Michael, and Sheila Jasanoff. 1998. "Contested Identities: Science, Law and Forensic Practice." *Social Studies of Science* 28(5–6): 675–86.

Lynch, Michael, and Ruth McNally. 2003. " 'Science,' 'Common Sense,' and DNA Evidence: A Legal Controversy about the Public Understanding of Science." *Public Understanding of Science* 12(1): 83–103.

Maeseele, Pieter, Daniëlle Raeijmaekers, Laurens Van der Steen, Robin Reul, and Steve Paulussen. 2017. "In Flanders Fields: De/Politicization and Democratic Debate on a GM Potato Field Trial Controversy in News Media." *Environmental Communication* 11(2): 166–83.

Magaldi Fernández, Adrián. 2019. "Reescribiendo La Transición. La Memoria Histórica y El Nuevo Relato de Las Élites." Pp. 155–66 in *Del siglo XIX al XXI: tendencias y debates.* Biblioteca Virtual Miguel de Cervantes.

Makarovs, Kirils, and Peter Achterberg. 2018. "Science to the People: A 32-Nation Survey." *Public Understanding of Science* 27(7): 876–96.

Marchart, Oliver. 2005. *Das Historisch-Politische Gedächtnis. Für Eine Politische Theorie Kollektiver Erinnerung.* Pp. 43–78 in *Memory in the 21st Century,* ed. Ljiljana Radonic and Heidemarie Uhl. Bielefeld: transcript Verlag.

Marcus, George E. 2012. "Multi-Sited Ethnography: Notes and Queries." Pp. 181–96 in *Multi-Sited Ethnography: Theory, Praxis, and Locality in Contemporary Research*. London: Ashgate.

de Mata, Ignacio Fernández. 2007. "El Surgimiento de La Memoria Histórica. Sentidos, Malentendidos y Disputas." Pp. 195–208 in *La Tradición Como Reclamo. Antropología En Castilla y León, Coordinado Por Luis Díaz y Pedro Tomé*. Salamanca: Consejería de Cultura y Turismo/Junta de Castilla y León.

de Mata, Ignacio Fernández. 2009. "In Memoriam . . . Esquelas, Contra-Esquelas y Duelos Inconclusos de La Guerra Civil Española." *Historia, Antropología y Fuentes Orales* 93–127.

Mbembé, J. A. 2003. "Necropolitics." *Public Culture* 15(1): 11–40.

McAdam, Doug. 1996. "Conceptual Origins, Current Problems, Future Directions." *Comparative Perspectives on Social Movements: Political Opportunities, Mobilizing Structures, and Cultural Framings* 23–40.

McCrudden, Christopher. 2008. "Human Dignity and Judicial Interpretation of Human Rights." *European Journal of International Law* 19(4): 655–724.

de Menezes, Alison Ribeiro. 2018. "The Necropolitics of Spain's Civil War Dead." Pp. 115–37 in *Public Humanities and the Spanish Civil War*. New York: Springer.

Michaels, Ralf. 2009. "Global Legal Pluralism." *Annual Review of Law and Social Science* 5: 243–62.

Michel, Verónica, and Kathryn Sikkink. 2013. "Human Rights Prosecutions and the Participation Rights of Victims in Latin America." *Law & Society Review* 47(4): 873–907.

Mihr, Anja. 2017. "An Introduction to Transitional Justice." *An Introduction to Transitional Justice* 1–28.

Molden, Berthold. 2016. "Resistant Pasts Versus Mnemonic Hegemony: On the Power Relations of Collective Memory." *Memory Studies* 9(2): 125–42.

Montoto Ugarte, Marina. 2014. "Una Mirada a La Crisis Del Relato Mítico de La Transición: La 'Querella Argentina' Contra Los Crímenes Del Franquismo." *Historia Actual Online* 3: 153–171.

Montoto Ugarte, Marina. 2019. "Un Viaje de Ida y Vuelta: La Construcción Social de La 'Víctima' En La Querella Argentina Contra Los Crímenes Del Franquismo." PhD thesis, Universidad Complutense de Madrid.

Moon, Claire. 2013. "Interpreters of the Dead: Forensic Knowledge, Human Remains and the Politics of the Past." *Social & Legal Studies* 22(2): 149–69.

Nauenberg, Saskia. 2015. "Spreading the Truth: How Truth Commissions Address Human Rights Abuses in the World Society." *International Sociology* 30(6): 654–73.

Navarro, Vicenç. 2008. "Los niños perdidos del franquismo." *El País*, December 23.

Neuman, Jeannette. 2017. "Spanish Vote Calling for Franco's Exhumation Revives Old Divisions." *The Wall Street Journal*, May 11.

Obledo, Micaela N. 2009. "Forensic Archeology in Criminal and Civil Cases." *Forensic Mag* 6(4): 31–34.

Oegema, Dirk, and Bert Klandermans. 1994. "Why Social Movement Sympathizers Don't Participate: Erosion and Nonconversion of Support." *American Sociological Review* 703–22.

Oreskes, Naomi. 2019. *Why Trust Science?* Princeton, NJ: Princeton University Press.

Oreskes, Naomi, and Erik M. Conway. 2011. *Merchants of Doubt: How a Handful of Scientists Obscured the Truth on Issues from Tobacco Smoke to Global Warming*. New York: Bloomsbury Publishing USA.

Pauchulo, Ana Laura. 2009. "Re-Telling the Story of Madres and Abuelas de Plaza de Mayo in Argentina: Lessons on Constructing Democracy and Reconstructing Memory." *Canadian Woman Studies* 27(1): 29–35.

Pepermans, Yves, and Pieter Maeseele. 2014. "Democratic Debate and Mediated Discourses on Climate Change: From Consensus to de/Politicization." *Environmental Communication* 8(2): 216–32.

Phelps, Teresa Godwin. 2014. "Truth Delayed: Accounting for Human Rights Violations in Guatemala and Spain." *Human Rights Quarterly* 36: 820.

Phillips Jr, William D., and Carla Rahn Phillips. 2015. *A Concise History of Spain*. Cambridge: Cambridge University Press.

Pradhan, Happy David. 2020. "A Critical Analysis of Transitional Justice and Rule of Law in Post-Authoritarian Democracies." Pp. 225–29 in *International Conference on Law Reform (INCLAR 2019)*. Paris: Atlantis.

Preston, Paul. 2002. *Franco*. Barcelona: Grijalbo.

Preston, Paul. 2007. *The Spanish Civil War: Reaction, Revolution and Revenge*. New York: Norton.

Preston, Paul. 2012. *The Spanish Holocaust: Inquisition and Extermination in Twentieth-Century Spain*. New York: Norton.

Prieto, José Luis. 2008. "La Antropología Forense En España Desde La Perspectiva de La Medicina Forense." *Cuadernos de Medicina Forense* 53(54): 189–200.

Raimundo, Filipa. 2012. "Post–Transitional Justice? Spain, Poland, and Portugal Compared." PhD thesis. Available at: https://www. researchgate. net /profile.

Rech, Fernando Serrulla. 2018. "Antropologia Forense de La Guerra Civil Española." PhD thesis, Universidad de Granada.

Renshaw, Layla. 2010. "Missing Bodies Near-at-Hand: The Dissonant Memory and Dormant Graves of the Spanish Civil War." Pp. 45–61 in *An Anthropology of Absence*. New York: Springer.

Renshaw, Layla. 2011. "Exhuming Loss." *Memory, Materiality and Mass Graves of the Spanish Civil War*. New York: Routledge.

Riessman, Catherine Kohler. 1994. *Qualitative Studies in Social Work Research*. London: SAGE.

Risse-Kappen, Thomas, Thomas Risse, Stephen C. Ropp, and Kathryn Sikkink. 1999. *The Power of Human Rights: International Norms and Domestic Change*. Vol. 66. Cambridge: Cambridge University Press.

Robben, Antonius C. G. M. 2000. "State Terror in the Netherworld." *Death Squad: The Anthropology of State Terror* 91.

Robben, Antonius C. G. M. 2015. "Exhumations, Territoriality, and Necropolitics in Chile and Argentina." Pp. 53–75 in *Necropolitics: Mass Graves and Exhumations in the Age of Human Rights*, ed. Francisco Ferrándiz and Antonius C. G. M. Robben. Philadelphia: University of Pennsylvania Press.

Robben, Antonius C. G. M., ed. 2017. *Death, Mourning, and Burial: A Cross-Cultural Reader*. New York: Wiley.

Rodríguez Arias, Miguel Ángel. 2008. "El Caso de Los Niños Perdidos Del Franquismo: Crimen Contra La Humanidad." *El Caso de Los Niños Perdidos Del Franquismo* 1–436.

Rose-Greenland, Fiona. 2014. "Looters, Collectors and a Passion for Antiquities at the Margins of Italian Society." *Journal of Modern Italian Studies* 19(5): 570–82.

Rosenblatt, Adam. 2015. *Digging for the Disappeared: Forensic Science After Atrocity*. Palo Alto, CA: Stanford University Press.

Rubin, Jonah S. 2014. "Transitional Justice Against the State: Lessons from Spanish Civil Society-Led Forensic Exhumations." *International Journal of Transitional Justice* 8(1): 99–120.

Rubin, Jonah S. 2015. "Technologies of the Afterlife: The Agency of the Dead at Spanish Mass Grave Exhumations." *Anthropological Journal of European Cultures* 24(1): 141–49.

Rubin, Jonah S. 2016. " 'They Are Not Just Bodies': Memory, Death, and Democracy in Post-Franco Spain." PhD thesis, The University of Chicago.

Rubin, Jonah S. 2018. "How Francisco Franco Governs from Beyond the Grave: An Infrastructural Approach to Memory Politics in Contemporary Spain." *American Ethnologist* 45(2): 214–27.

Rubin, Jonah S. 2020. "Exhuming Dead Persons: Forensic Science and the Making of Post-Fascist Publics in Spain." *Cultural Anthropology* 35(3): 345–73.

Ruibal, Alfredo González. 2008. "Arqueología de la Guerra Civil Española." *Complutum* 19: 10.

Ryan, Lorraine. 2017. "Memory, Transnational Justice, and Recession in Contemporary Spain." *European Review* 25(2): 295–306.

Sanford, Victoria. 2003. *Buried Secrets: Truth and Human Rights in Guatemala.* New York: Palgrave Macmillan.

Schweitzer, Nicholas J., and Michael J. Saks. 2007. "The CSI Effect: Popular Fiction About Forensic Science Affects the Public's Expectations about Real Forensic Science." *Jurimetrics* 357–64.

Shaw, Ian, and Nick Gould. 2001. *Qualitative Social Work Research.* London: SAGE.

Sikkink, Kathryn, and Carrie Booth Walling. 2007. "The Impact of Human Rights Trials in Latin America." *Journal of Peace Research* 44(4): 427–45.

Sikkink, Kathryn. 2011. *The Justice Cascade: How Human Rights Prosecutions Are Changing World Politics (The Norton Series in World Politics).* New York: Norton.

Sikkink, Kathryn. 2019. "The Emergence, Evolution, and Effectiveness of the Latin American Human Rights Network." Pp. 59–84 in *Constructing Democracy.* New York: Routledge.

Silva, Emilio. 2005. *Las Fosas de Franco: Crónica de Un Desagravio.* Barcelona: Temas de Hoy.

Smith, Lindsay Adams. 2016. "Identifying Democracy: Citizenship, DNA, and Identity in Postdictatorship Argentina." *Science, Technology, & Human Values* 41(6): 1037–62.

Snow, David A., and Robert D. Benford. 1988. "Ideology, Frame Resonance and Participant Mobilization." Pp. 197–218 in, *From Structure to Action: Comparing Social Movement Across Cultures,* ed. Bert Klandermans, Hanspeter Kriesi, and Sidney Tarrow. London: Jai.

Snow, David A., E. Burke Rochford Jr, Steven K. Worden, and Robert D. Benford. 1986. "Frame Alignment Processes, Micromobilization, and Movement Participation." *American Sociological Review* 464–81.

Snyder, Cindy S., Wesley J. Gabbard, J. Dean May, and Nihada Zulcic. 2006. "On the Battleground of Women's Bodies: Mass Rape in Bosnia-Herzegovina." *Affilia* 21(2): 184–95.

Spain, Amnesty International. May 23, 2017. "Exhumación De Fosa Común En El Cementerio De Guadalajara." *YouTube*.

Specht, Annie R. 2013. "Killer Corn and Capitalist Pigs: Forensic Noir and Television Portrayals of Modern Agricultural Technology." *Culture, Agriculture, Food and Environment* 35(2): 152–61.

Stambolis-Ruhstorfer, Michael. 2015. "The Culture of Knowledge: Constructing 'Expertise' in Legal Debates on Marriage and Kinship for Same-Sex Couples in France and the United States." PhD thesis, UCLA.

Tarrow, Sidney. 2001. "Transnational Politics: Contention and Institutions in International Politics." *Annual Review of Political Science* 4(1): 1–20.

Tarrow, Sidney. 2005. *The New Transnational Activism*. Cambridge: Cambridge University Press.

Taylor, Telford. 1993. *The Anatomy of the Nuremberg Trials: A Personal Memoir*. New York: Knopf.

Thomas, Hugh. 2001. *The Spanish Civil War*. London: Penguin Random House.

Toom, Victor, R. Hindmash, and B. Prainsack. n.d. "Genetic Suspects. Global Governance of Forensic DNA Profiling and Databasing." Pp. 175–196 in *Inquisitorial Forensic DNA Profiling in the Netherlands and the Expansion of the Forensic Genetic Body*. Cambridge: Cambridge University Press.

Torrús, Alejandro. 2020. "Familias, Asociaciones e Instituciones Han Recuperado Los Cuerpos de Más de 9.000 Republicanos de Fosas Comunes Hasta 2018." *Público*, August 15.

Ugarte, Marina Montoto. 2017. "Las Víctimas Del Franquismo En 'La Querella Argentina': Luchas Por El Reconocimiento y Nuevas Desigualdades." *Papeles Del CEIC. International Journal on Collective Identity Research* (1): 1–25.

Ugarte, Marina Montoto. 2020. " 'Nosotros También Somos Víctimas': Las Luchas Por La Justicia y El Reconocimiento de Las Víctimas Del Franquismo En La Querella Argentina1." *Revista de Antropología Social* 29(2): 199–211.

Verdery, Katherine. 1999. *The Political Lives of Dead Bodies: Reburial and Post-socialist Change*. New York: Columbia University Press.

Vinitsky-Seroussi, Vered. 2002. "Commemorating a Difficult Past: Yitzhak Rabin's Memorials." *American Sociological Review* 67: 30–51.

Wagner, Sarah. 2008. *To Know Where He Lies: DNA Technology and the Search for Srebrenica's Missing*. Berkeley: University of California Press.

Waylen, Georgina. 1994. "Women and Democratization Conceptualizing Gender Relations in Transition Politics." *World Politics* 46(3): 327–54.

Webb, Brian S., and Doug Hayhoe. 2017. "Assessing the Influence of an Educational Presentation on Climate Change Beliefs at an Evangelical Christian College." *Journal of Geoscience Education* 65(3): 272–82.

Whitlinger, Claire. 2015. "From Countermemory to Collective Memory: Acknowledging the 'Mississippi Burning' Murders." *Sociological Forum* 30(51): 648–70.

Wilson, Richard J. 1999. "Prosecuting Pinochet: International Crimes in Spanish Domestic Law." *Human Rights Quarterly* 927–79.

Zapico Barbeito, Mónica. 2010. "La Investigación de Los Crímenes Del Franquismo: Entre El Procesamiento Por Prevaricación Abierto Contra El Juez Baltasar Garzón y La Querella Presentada En Argentina En Virtud Del Ejercicio de La Jurisdicción Universal." *Anuario da Facultade de Dereito da Universidade da Coruña* 14: 891–927.

Zawodny, J. K. 2015 [1962]. *Death in the Forest; The Story of the Katyn Forest Massacre*. Auckland: Pickle Partners.

Zerubavel, Eviatar. 2006. *The Elephant in the Room: Silence and Denial in Everyday Life*. Oxford: Oxford University Press.

Zimmerman, Bill, Rita Arditti, Pat Brennan, and Steven Cavrak. 1980. "People's Science." *Science and Liberation* 299–319.

Zubrzycki, Geneviève. 2017. *National Matters: Materiality, Culture, and Nationalism*. Stanford University Press.

INDEX

GPSR Authorized Representative: Easy Access System Europe, Mustamäe tee
50, 10621 Tallinn, Estonia, gpsr.requests@easproject.com

www.ingramcontent.com/pod-product-compliance
Lightning Source LLC
Chambersburg PA
CBHW021859020426
42334CB00013B/393